CARE OF THE ELDERLY

Pergamon Titles of Related Interest

Lewinsohn/Teri CLINICAL GEROPSYCHOLOGY: New Directions in
Assessment and Treatment
Tamir COMMUNICATION AND THE AGING PROCESS: Interaction
Throughout the Life Cycle
Yost/Beutler/Corbishley/Allender GROUP COGNITIVE THERAPY:
A Treatment Method for the Depressed Elderly

Related Journals*

CLINICAL PSYCHOLOGY REVIEW
EXPERIMENTAL GERONTOLOGY

*Free specimen copies available upon request.

PSYCHOLOGY PRACTITIONER GUIDEBOOKS

EDITORS

Arnold P. Goldstein, Syracuse University
Leonard Krasner, SUNY at Stony Brook
Sol L. Garfield, Washington University

CARE OF THE ELDERLY
A Family Approach

ELSIE M. PINKSTON
University of Chicago
NATHAN L. LINSK
University of Illinois at Chicago

PERGAMON PRESS
New York   Oxford   Toronto   Sydney   Paris   Frankfurt

Pergamon Press Offices:

U.S.A.   Pergamon Press Inc., Maxwell House, Fairview Park,
                     Elmsford, New York 10523, U.S.A.

U.K.   Pergamon Press Ltd., Headington Hill Hall,
                     Oxford OX3 0BW, England

CANADA   Pergamon Press Canada Ltd., Suite 104, 150 Consumers Road,
                     Willowdale, Ontario M2J 1P9, Canada

AUSTRALIA   Pergamon Press (Aust.) Pty. Ltd., P.O. Box 544,
                     Potts Point, NSW 2011, Australia

FRANCE   Pergamon Press SARL, 24 rue des Ecoles,
                     75240 Paris, Cedex 05, France

FEDERAL REPUBLIC Pergamon Press GmbH, Hammerweg 6,
OF GERMANY   D-6242 Kronberg-Taunus, Federal Republic of Germany

Library of Congress Cataloging in Publication Data

Pinkston, Elsie M.
    Care of the elderly.

    Bibiography: p.
    Includes index.
    1. Aged--Home care. 2. Aged--Family relationships.
3. Behavior modification. I. Linsk, Nathan L.
II. Title.
RA564.8.P56   1984   362.6   84-11056
ISBN 0-08-030978-X
ISBN 0-08-030977-1 (pbk.)

Printed in the United States of America

Contents

List of Tables   viii

List of Figures   ix

Preface   x

Chapter

1. TEACHING BEHAVIORAL FAMILY TREATMENT
   TO PRACTITIONERS   1

2. PRACTICE AND RESEARCH WITH THE ELDERLY   5
   Support of the Elderly   6
   Behavioral Gerontology   8
   Family Training as Caregivers   9
   Linkage with Community Services   10
   Summary   11

3. ASSESSMENT OF CLIENT PROBLEMS
   AND RESOURCES   13
   The Behavioral Paradigm   15
   Personal Variables   16
   The Prosthetic Environment   20
   Assessment Components   20
       Assessment Interviews   20
       Problem Selection   23

| | Observations | 24 |
| | Indirect Measures | 29 |

4.   INTERVENTION PROCEDURES AND GUIDELINES   33
        The Caregiver   34
        Goals   35
        Behavior Change Strategies   35
            Increasing Opportunities for Reinforcement   36
            Increasing Behaviors   38
            Decreasing Behaviors   39
        Training and Delivery Systems   41
            Educating the Caregiver   42
            Delivery Systems   43
        Planning for Maintenance of Change   44
            Fading   45
            Environmental Reprogramming   46
            Program Transfer   47
        Community Service Linkages   47
            When to Link   48
            Linkage Procedures   49
            Sources of Service Linkage Information 49
        Termination and Follow-up   49

5.   EVALUATION OF INTERVENTION
     AS A PRACTICE INNOVATION   51
        Clinical Baseline Intervention Comparison 52
            Clinical Multiple-Baseline Intervention 53
            Intervention-Reversal Design   53
        Changing-Criteria Designs   55
        Multiple-Baseline-Across-Behaviors -Design 55
        Multiple-Baseline-Across-Settings Design 56
        Multiple-Baseline-Across-Clients Design   56
        Multiple-Replication Design   56
        Summary   57

6.   APPLICATION OF BEHAVIORAL PROCEDURES
     TO SPECIFIC PROBLEMS   58
        Increasing Social Contacts   58
            Practice Illustration 1: Using Contracts to Increase
            Independence and Social Contacts
            Practitioner/Researchers: Glenn R. Green,
            and Christine Marlow   60

Improving Self-Care   64
Practice Illustration 2: Promoting Self-Care
with an Older Couple
Practitioner/Researcher: Glenn R. Green   66
Practice Illustration 3: Improving Independent
Elimination
Practitioner/Researcher: Rosemary Nelson Young   69
Improving Verbal Behavior   73
Practice Illustration 4: Reduction of Problem
Verbalizations
Practitioner/Researcher: John Schipke   76
Improving Multiple Problems   79
Practice Illustration 5: Improving Family
Interaction and Personal Care for an
Elderly Depressed Man
Practitioner/Researcher: Rosemary Nelson Young   80
Practice Illustration 6: Reducing Reported
Hallucinations and Improving Activities
Practitioner/Researcher: Judy N. Jacobi   85

7.   SUMMARY: THE MODEL AND ITS USES   91
Model Summary   92
Evaluation   93
Role and Setting Considerations   95
Summary   95

Bibliography   96

References   101

Author Index   107

Subject Index   111

About the Authors   115

Psychology Practitioner Guidebooks List   116

List of Tables

Table 3.1	Referral Procedures	17
Table 3.2	Caregiver Checklist	17
Table 3.3	Dos and Don'ts for Interviewing Older Clients	21
Table 3.4	Interview Guide to Assess Problem Behavior	23
Table 3.5	Anecdotal Record	25
Table 4.1	Intervention Selection Guidelines	42
Table 5.1	Single-Case Designs	54
Table 6.1	Intervention Procedures: Increasing Social Contacts	59
Table 6.2	Intervention Procedures: Self-Care Behavior	65
Table 6.3	Intervention Procedures: Elimination Program	71
Table 6.4	Intervention Procedures: Decreasing Negative Verbalizations	75

List of Figures

Figure 3.1	Activity Record	28
Figure 3.2	Family Behavior Record	30
Figure 6.1	Task Assignment Work Sheet (selected entries)	62
Figure 6.2	Mrs. Banks' Weekly Frequency of Visitors and Telephone Calls	63
Figure 6.3	Self-care Forms	67
Figure 6.4	Mrs. Thomas' Sugar Checks	68
Figure 6.5	Filled-in Activity Record	70
Figure 6.6	Mr. Raven's Urination Behavior	72
Figure 6.7	Verbal Behavior Record: Mr. Brooks	77
Figure 6.8	Mr. Brooks' Frequency of Positive and Worried Statements per Day	78
Figure 6.9	Mr. Keller's Multi-intervention Program	82
Figure 6.10	Mr. Walters' Daily Activities	87

Preface

During the past few years the elderly population has increased greatly in the United States, and concurrently there has been a movement to help elderly people remain at home as long as possible by providing home health care, home delivered meals, and other supplements to their care. The Elderly Support Project was developed to fill yet another need: care of older people with special mental and physical disabilities. This program was designed to teach family caregivers additional skills for enriching the quality of life for elderly people by using behavior management techniques, which include reinforcement, cues, and redesigning the physical environment to facilitate better behavioral functioning.

The following chapters are designed to train practitioners to teach family caregivers better skills for care of the elderly; particularly how to resolve behavior problems resulting from brain damage, too few appropriate consequences for maintenance of behaviors, and prolonged hospital care with its resulting stimulus deprivation. These family-training procedures are an indirect replication of those used with other dependent populations requiring a high degree of care such as children with behavior problems or retarded and disabled people.

These chapters are components of a larger model and describe the problems of the impaired elderly, the methods for assessing those problems, interventions for those problems, methods of evaluating those interventions, and examples of interventions using behavioral procedures with clients. Many example forms are provided to aid practitioners in implementing the program.

This is a book for practitioners, students, professionals, and paraprofessionals. Essentially, anyone who plans to visit the homes of the elderly for the purposes of intervention with their problems could benefit from this book. The practice illustrations were conducted by people in nonacademic settings; that is, at homes of clients and in cooperation with public and private agencies and hospitals. Workshops have been conducted with the staffs of these institutions, and they have successfully used these procedures with their clients.

Our intellectual debt, as always, is to Donald M. Baer and his colleagues at the Department of Human Development at The University of Kansas, but in recent years we have also been touched and inspired by the way that our earlier leaders, Fred Keller and B. F. Skinner, have practiced what they preached as they employed behavioral techniques to maintain their quality of life while growing older.

The research that provided the basis for this manual was supported by the Illinois Department of Mental Health and Developmental Disabilities (IDMHDD) (Grant Number 8065-03) and the National Institute on Aging (Grant Number RO1 AGO2612). We would particularly like to thank Louis Aarons of IDMHDD for his encouragement in pursuing this research. The cooperation of the Illinois State Psychiatric Institute was rendered by Lawrence W. Lazarus, MD, Jerald Lessor, MD, and Rhoda Frankel, ACSW.

The project was conducted at the School of Social Service Administration at The University of Chicago. Our colleagues Sheldon S. Tobin, PhD, Jeanne Marsh, PhD, and John Schuerman, PhD, assisted us in planning our strategies.

Several hospitals and service agencies contributed by providing referrals and staff consultation regarding community service resources. These included Jackson Park Hospital, the Rehabilitation Institute of Chicago, Johnston R. Bowman Health Center for the Elderly, and The University of Chicago Hospitals. Robert Kahn, PhD, and Allen Kodish, MD of The University of Chicago Gerontology Clinic were helpful in developing the research and clinical components.

We wish to acknowledge the participation and patience of our clients, both the elderly and their families, especially during the developmental stages of the research.

We would like to emphasize that this is a group effort and to express our gratitude to those who assisted in the development of these procedures and the preparation of this book.

Our primary acknowledgement is to Glenn R. Green for his collaboration on the original research from which these methods and procedures were drawn and who generously contributed early drafts of the methods and procedures included in this book.

The practitioner/researchers were responsible for the illustrations in this book and contributed to all aspects of this work. We are very proud of the role they continue to play in the mental health community. Glenn R. Green (PhD, The University of Chicago) is the Executive Director of The

Proviso Council on Aging in Bellwood, Illinois. Rosemary Nelson Young (MA, The University of Chicago) is the Project Director of the Elderly Support Project, and supervises training of practitioner/researchers and procedural guideline development. John Schipke (MA, The University of Chicago) is a counselor at Group Health Inc. in St. Paul, Minnesota. Christine Marlow (PhD, University of Chicago) is an Assistant Professor, Indiana University, Bloomington, Indiana. Judy N. Jacobi (MPH, University of Pittsburgh) is Director of Information and Referral Services, Swanson Mental Health Center, La Porte, Indiana.

Eric Rankin, Barbara Strauss, and N. Dawn Isis assisted in data analysis.

Steven Roskamp, Robin S. Goldberg, Patricia Hanrahan, and Irene Wade provided valuable assistance on the production of the document. Grace Levit served as content editor, and editorial assistance was provided by Beverlee E. Silva and Eleanora Keane-Hagerty. Their candor greatly improved this book.

Finally, we would like to thank Robert E. McKenna and Leah Linsk, who made our lives full, rich, and fun by reminding us that there is a good time to be had and insisting that we have it.

Chapter 1
Teaching Behavioral Family Treatment to Practitioners

This book contains specific procedures designed to aid practitioners who teach family caregivers the skills that promote high-quality care for declining elderly people.[1] The training procedures, which are similar to those tested by Patterson, Forehand, Pinkston, and other behaviorists, include modeling, corrective feedback, rehearsal, and reinforcement. The explicit intervention techniques use behavioral interventions and specific community-service linkages to improve home care. Functional analysis and a combination of contracting, stimulus cues, and reinforcement-based interventions comprise the most highly developed and evaluated interventions. For the most common problems, such as urinary incontinence, low-rate activities, bizarre verbal behavior, and self-care deficits, step-by-step instructions are presented that include procedures for evaluation and revision of each intervention. These procedures represent an application of parent-training techniques derived from operant theory and adapted to elderly people and their families. When applied to the elderly, these explicit procedures are generally effective and show lasting change (Linsk, Pinkston, & Green, 1982; Pinkston & Linsk, in press).

Using this guidebook, practitioners will learn how to teach caregivers to improve the supportive aspects of the social and physical environments of older people and thereby promote higher quality home care. Families will learn how to solve their individual problems using a tested service model, which is based on social-learning, operant, and case-management approaches. By following the training procedures, practitioners teach caregivers to specify desirable and undesirable behaviors related to social and

[1]Throughout this book elderly people are called *clients* and their family members or friends are called *caregivers*.

1

health problems. Caregivers then learn to use behavioral procedures, such as stimulus cueing and reinforcement, to increase the frequency of desired behavior of older people as well as the opportunity for gratifying experiences. Practitioners also teach families how to obtain appropriate community services that provide additional resources for the enrichment of clients' quality of life. Assessment and intervention efforts by practitioners are scheduled in clients' homes for 10 or 15 sessions per client. Additional procedures are introduced to enhance maintenance and for necessary program modifications in the initial plan. A follow-up assessment is conducted to determine the effectiveness of these procedures in achieving maintenance.

These methods emphasize (a) the utility of an individualized measured approach, (b) the efficacy of informal support in treating behavior problems associated with institutionalization, (c) the value of integrating behavioral training procedures and operationalized linkage procedures for increasing social involvement and decreasing psychiatric complaints, and (d) the importance of ongoing assessment to determine program effectiveness and the appropriateness of modifications.

The program method is divided into seven steps: (a) referral, (b) assessment, (c) definition of behaviors and recording of baseline data, (d) behavioral education of support persons, (e) design of intervention, (f) termination and maintenance, and (g) follow-up. All of the steps are important, but the acquisition and maintenance of positive behavioral effects are essential and are integrated into all parts of the program.

The client, the caregiver, and the practitioner use assessment, an integral part of treatment, to design and revise the intervention. Each client's program is assessed daily, using standardized and individualized instruments. Progress is measured by comparing records of the client's postintervention behavior with baseline data. Preintervention and postintervention questionnaires are used to assess the client's ability to perform daily life tasks and to interact with others at home and in the community. Direct observation measures, recorded by the caregiver and, at times, the client, and indirect measures of functioning and attitudes also aid in evaluation and revision of intervention procedures. Evaluation throughout all aspects of the program helps to establish valid treatment methods.

The procedures in this book are based on the findings of a research and service project conducted by the staff of the Elderly Support Project (ESP) and funded by state and federal grants.

The broader purpose of this guidebook is to present a model for assisting older people who are no longer able to meet their own personal and social needs because of age-related physical and psychological changes. Clients appropriate for these services are age 60 or more, tend to be socially isolated, and exhibit diminished capacity for personal care and other daily life tasks. Many have limited mobility due to physical disabilities such as arthritis and cardiovascular problems. They also have intellectual or emotional difficulties or disorders, including clinical diagnoses of organic brain syndromes, depression, and paranoia, as well as a range of physical impairments. Behavioral deficits and excesses take the form of low rates of socialization, limited regular activities, eating disorders, exercise deficiencies, wandering, destructive acts, excessive smoking, argumentative or bizarre speech or excessive complaining, deficient self-care behaviors, or any combination of these traits. These behaviors often result in an increased risk of relocation or institutionalization. Moreover, they decrease rates of interaction with the community. This further reduces pleasurable activities by limiting access to stimulating situations where social intercourse and friendship might be found; that is, access to reinforcers is decreased.

A range of caregivers and of clients with behavior problems have been treated in this project. During the referral process the client and caregiver characteristics are matched to criteria established by research evaluation. Client criteria are the following conditions:

- An age of over 60 years.
- Diagnoses of psychological problems and/or brain dysfunction, including chronic and acute brain syndromes, reactive mental disorders, depressions that prevent community functioning, senile psychosis, paraphrenia, arteriosclerotic brain disease, and acute confusional states. Physical impairments included cardiovascular accidents, arthritis, fracture, and spinal cord injury.
- Excessive disability; that is, functional disability greater than that warranted by health status (Kahn, 1965).
- A caregiver available to participate in behavioral change efforts.
- Behavioral excesses or deficits in rates of appropriate or inappropriate behavior, family interaction dysfunction, interpersonal problems, communication difficulties, social isolation, or inability to engage in activities of daily living and low rates of interaction with community activity.

Caregiver characteristics appropriate to the program are derived from criteria believed necessary for implementing a behavioral intervention. Because the caregivers are involved in all aspects of the assessment and intervention, it is important that they have basic skills and motivation for participation. The following criteria are recommended for the selection of caregivers:

- Have adequate time and commitment for involvement with the program.
- Have adequate motivation, that is, are affected by the behavior of the client and have ongoing contact.

- Have adequate access to the client and control of social consequences of the client's behaviors.
- Demonstrate adequate skill levels or ability to learn skills.
- Demonstrate adequate mental and physical health for participation.

Demographic variables such as age, relationship, kinship, income, and other resources were monitored but were not used as criteria for selection. The caregivers in the project were usually family members, frequently spouses, with an average age of 75 years. All were willing to devote a certain amount of time to working directly with the client.

This program was tested with clients and caregivers who met the criteria just discussed. The procedures improved long-term functioning and decreased the likelihood of institutional care for many of the clients. This was particularly true with older people whose behavioral deficits were in excess of their physical disabilities. These procedures successfully improved the support systems of both the clients and their caregivers, thus decreasing family stress. Generally the behavioral improvements were maintained over time, as shown by 6-month and yearly assessments.

Families usually regarded the program as helpful, viewed the data recording and corrective feedback as important, and found their participation in the design and implementation of the intervention procedures rewarding.

In summary, this behavioral treatment program employs families to enhance the informal client supports, to implement linkage procedures to formal support services, and to improve service coordination. Treatment and linkage procedures facilitate joint planning among older persons, their families and other support persons, and practitioners, to build sustaining systems for older people.

Chapter 2

Practice and Research with the Elderly

The methods discussed here for treating elderly people by working cooperatively with their families and caregivers are based on the assumptions that (a) families are frequently participants in the care of the elderly, (b) behavioral gerontology and behavioral family-training methods are effective, and (c) community linkages to additional supports are necessary in many instances. These methods were developed by working with families willing to spend time to improve the care of their elderly members. This chapter reviews family involvement patterns, highlights innovative service programs, and briefly examines behavioral gerontology and family-training programs. The following case is representative of the families that were treated with the procedures in this guidebook.

Mr. DeBerry lived with his daughter in her home. He experienced difficulty walking because of arthritic pain, frequently did not arrive at the bathroom in time to urinate properly, had trouble keeping track of which day it was, and exhibited other memory problems. He had just completed an extensive medical and psychiatric evaluation and received a diagnosis of senile dementia. The helplessness and irreversibility suggested by this diagnosis provoked fear in both the daughter and the father. As clients of the Elderly Support Project, they were taught to use a simple schedule for elimination, to use communication cues to enhance the father's memory abilities, and to encourage better and more frequent walking by using a schedule and praising compliance to a walking contract. Mr. DeBerry and his daughter are typical of families that can be taught simple procedures to alleviate certain of the behavior problems of old age.

The elderly are not a homogeneous group, and it is seldom appropriate to use age as the major criterion for categorizing people or for approaches to help them. Age is usually a less relevant characteristic than mental, physical, or behavioral functioning. Diagnostic categories often add a new, unattractive label and have little reliability. (For a discussion of diagnosis in the elderly, see Butler & Lewis, 1982, chap. 9.) Impaired elders are easily stereotyped by diagnostic categories based on a medical model that tends to emphasize personality and biological characteristics of individuals over behavioral interactions within their social and physical environments. Only 2% to 3% of persons over 65 are mentally impaired or disoriented (Busse & Pfeiffer, 1969). Many problems, then, are a result of functional deficits, as opposed to irreversible mental and physical impairments. To help these people, it is useful to examine the environmental stimulation for and social consequences of behaviors. Behavioral interventions for the elderly emphasize the addition of environmental cues and the provision of more positive consequences for behaviors. The goal for practitioners is to teach the elderly and their caregivers different ways of initiating and responding to each other and procedures to reestablish appropriate behaviors that have been eliminated from the elderly person's repertoire following temporary illness.

SUPPORT OF THE ELDERLY

Although the frequency of family assistance to elderly relatives has been questioned, recent studies have emphasized the widespread existence of family help patterns (Levit, 1978; Shanas, 1960, 1978; Sussman, 1965; Treas, 1977). Assistance to older relatives varies according to interaction patterns, economic resources, and competing demands on time (Brody, Poulshock, & Masciocchi, 1978). Family-provided service is diverse and includes assistance with activities of daily living (self-care), financial help, household help, errands, direct care, and ongoing supervision (Kulys & Tobin, 1980). Although often overlooked, 8% of men and 16% of women over age 65 live in homes of family members (General Accounting Office, 1977). This percentage increases with age and disability (Bussink, Van der Tak, & Zuga, 1976). Apparently, older people are recipients of considerable family assistance when strong relationships with relatives exist prior to functional losses (Brody, 1967; Brody et al., 1978; Sussman, 1965). Maddox (1975) cited the absence of helping family as a critical factor in institutionalization, a finding supported by others (Barney, 1977; Tobin & Lieberman, 1976; Townsend, 1965). Family presence is frequently more important than disability levels in predicting whether disabled elderly return to their homes or are institutionalized following hospitalization (Brody et al., 1978). These data suggest that family support programs and services are important components of providing home care to chronically ill or disabled elderly.

Although family assistance provisions vary, problems accompanying such efforts may occur due to competing demands for scarce familial resources (Rapoport, Rapoport, & Strelitz, 1970; Treas, 1977). Middle-aged family members are often faced with the burden of caring for their own children, themselves, and their aged parents at a time when they begin to experience the first evidence of their own aging (Goldfarb, 1965). Family assistance burdens may lead to both psychological and physical deterioration of the younger family members (Grad de Alarcon, Sainsbury, & Costain, 1975; Safford, 1977), financial concerns, (Sussman, 1979) or anger, rejection, or physical abuse (Kosberg, 1979; Lau & Kosberg, 1978; Rathbone-McCuan, 1980). These dysfunctional patterns suggest questions regarding the ability of family members to encourage older relatives to regain optimum functioning. Despite considerable discussion of the advantages of keeping the older person in the community (Morris, 1971; Tobin & Lieberman, 1976; White House Conference on Aging, 1973), there have been few attempts to develop specific techniques for building family supports to achieve this goal.

Preliminary suggestions for teaching family members to interact with and assist elderly relatives include group programs for families in family service agencies and homes for the aged. These groups have generally focused on physical and psychological components of aging, family reactions, and community resources (Brandwein & Postoff, 1977; Safford, 1977; Schier, 1972; Silverman, Kahn, & Anderson, 1977; Zimmer, Gross-Andrew, & Frankfather, 1977). Another source of information and involvement for families is self-help books designed for family caregivers (Bumagin & Hirn, 1979; Cohen & Gans, 1978; Otten & Shelley, 1976; Schwartz, 1977; Silverstone & Hyman, 1976).

Programs that provide more individualized services have recently been reported (Eisdorfer, 1980; Frankfather, Smith, & Caro, 1981; Zarit, Reever, & Weston, 1980). These programs are only beginning to personalize plans to promote specific family interventions. Although these efforts offer beginning tools for family assistance to older persons, they are based primarily on clinical wisdom, and their suggestions have not been subjected to rigorous methods of testing results. Seldom do these programs offer specific methods to enable families to maximize the social and behavioral potential of older family members. Keller and Hughston (1981) and Haley (1983) did delineate a variety of intervention possibilities that might prove helpful after additional evaluation of these techniques is completed.

The theoretical and practical framework for a family-based behavioral intervention system for the elderly emerges from three trends of research and service delivery: (a) behavioral gerontology, (b) behavioral parent and family-training techniques, and (c) community service linkage technology. These are combined to form a simple comprehensive treatment model.

BEHAVIORAL GERONTOLOGY

The problems of the mentally and physically impaired elderly have been analyzed from a behavioral perspective (Skinner, 1983). Lindsley (1964) specified the interrelationship between deficit behaviors of aging persons and environmental shortcomings in terms of appropriate discriminate stimuli and opportunities for reinforcement. This analysis calls for the provision of therapeutic consequences and prosthetic approaches to the problems of the elderly. Hoyer and his colleagues also described the behavioral context of problems of the elderly in terms of the physical and social environment (Hoyer, Mishara, & Reidel, 1975; Rebok & Hoyer, 1977). The more recent behavioral gerontology literature includes reports of the analysis and design of living environments for the elderly (Bayne, 1971; Hussian, 1981; Kastenbaum, 1968; MacDonald, 1978; McClannahan & Risley, 1974) and discussions of the advantages of a behavioral approach to treatment of the impaired elderly (Cautela, 1966; Cautela & Mansfield, 1977; Page, 1978; Shedletsky, 1977; Woods & Britton, 1977).

Fortunately, a wide range of behaviors of older people have been analyzed, treated, and evaluated, and they provide a bank of treatment procedures. In this guidebook, behaviors of older persons are classified into categories of self-care, negative activities and verbalizations, positive behaviors, and social contacts. Programs to treat problems in these behavior categories have been developed, particularly in residential institutions (see the bibliography).

Programs have been formulated to improve self-care behaviors including eating, dressing, elimination, and walking. Eating problems were treated using positive reinforcement, and modeling and feedback (Baltes & Zerbe, 1976; Blackman, Gehle, & Pinkston, 1979). Self-dressing was enhanced by providing materials, prompts, and cues. A number of techniques using schedules and reinforcement procedures were developed to intervene with incontinent elderly people (Grosicki, 1968; Howe, 1975; Schwartz & Blackman, 1976). Walking was increased by redesigning the environment and adding prosthetic devices as well as using reinforcement procedures (MacDonald & Butler, 1974). Additional personal care behaviors which have been treated or investigated include brushing teeth, bathing, and sleeping.

A number of programs were developed that focus on reducing negative behaviors such as self-injurious actions (Mishara, Robertson, & Kastenbaum, 1973) and repetitive movements. Tardive dyskinetic movements were effectively reduced using differential reinforcement of incompatible activities (Albanese & Gaarder, 1977; Jackson, 1980).

Programs to increase positive activities included adherence to medical regimen, physical exercise, and activity programs. Participation in activities in long-term care or hospital settings was the objective of several interventions. For instance, by comparing a number of motivating procedures,

McClannahan found that a combination of discriminative cues and rein-forcement most effectively increased participation in structured activities and that program materials were effective stimuli that encouraged such participation (1973). Hoyer and his colleagues also examined participation as a component of studies of specific verbal response increases (Hoyer, Mishara, & Reidel, 1975; Hoyer, Kafer, Simpson, & Hoyer, 1974). Black-man, Howe, and Pinkston (1976) made access to food a reinforcing con-sequence for participation in proximal social behavior. Linsk, Howe, and Pinkston (1975) demonstrated how teaching a practitioner to ask more questions could increase attending and talking by impaired elders in social group work programs. Linsk (1978) studied the effects of a program that prompted participation in outdoor activites. Levendusky (1978) demon-strated the need for corrective feedback to improve task behaviors of those attending a sheltered workshop for the elderly. All of these techniques may be useful to families concerned about increasing social participation of the community-residing elderly.

Social and verbal behaviors have been treated to improve quality of life within geriatric institutions (Baltes & Barton, 1977; Hoyer, 1973). Inap-propriate verbalizations have been decreased through the use of differen-tial attention techniques. Linsk and his colleagues (1975) successfully developed methods to increase verbal participation with extremely withdrawn and impaired elderly people in a home for the aged. In addi-tion, interpersonal skill-training procedures, including behavioral com-ponents, have been used to teach communication, negotiation, and social skills to nursing home residents.

Strategies have been suggested to enhance memory, improve orienta-tion, and reduce confusion (Eisdorfer, Cohen, & Preston, 1978). Behavioral research evaluated remotivation therapy (Taepfer, Bucknell, & Shaw, 1974) and reality orientation (Bernstein & Dvorkin, 1978). The results regarding the effectiveness of these approaches were inconclusive or negative.

In summary, a diverse array of behavioral techniques were developed and evaluated for use with older persons. Since 1968 most of this work has occurred within psychiatric hospitals or long-term nursing facilities. Application of these methods to community settings is incomplete. Whereas institutional staff have generally been the primary engineers of behavioral change, application to home settings requires that families be trained to successfully apply behavioral techniques.

FAMILY TRAINING AS CAREGIVERS

As treatment of developmental and behavioral disorders is shifting from the mental health or long-term care institution to community agencies and persons within the immediate environment, families are emerging as a primary resource for extending home care. Although self-management programs have been used successfully with older clients (Bellucci & Hoyer, 1975; Malemed, 1975; Meichenbaum, 1974; Page, 1978; Wheeler & Knight, 1981), many older people are unable to act as their own caregivers or support persons. In such cases the family becomes the focus.

The major source of information regarding behavioral family intervention is the parent-training literature. Parent-training methods use reinforcement techniques and environmental management procedures to achieve and maintain improvement (Patterson, Shaw, & Ebner, 1969; Tharp & Wetzel, 1969). Research has resulted in families being widely accepted by behaviorists as active participants in children's therapy (Berkowitz & Graziano, 1972; Johnson & Katz, 1973; O'Dell, 1974).

Behavioral parent training includes several aspects of treatment and experimentation which are relevant to family-based care of older people: (a) use of currently accepted behavioral treatment procedures and their effects, (b) use of the home setting for family education and intervention, (c) treatment of a wide range of behavior and socialization problems concerning diverse family members, (d) specific procedures for training parents, and (e) a well-developed evaluation methodology.

The intervention model described in this guidebook was adapted from a parent-training program developed by Elsie Pinkston and her colleagues for the treatment of young children (Pinkston, 1984; Pinkston, Friedman, & Polster, 1981; Pinkston, Levitt, Green, Linsk, & Rzepnicki, 1982); and it is based on social-reinforcement theory, with an emphasis on modeling and reinforcement. Practitioners teach family members procedures to increase their rates of positive reinforcement for positive behaviors involving interpersonal relations, household activities, and general functioning.

These research and practice findings demonstrate that parents (i.e., in this case family members) can be taught through instructions, contracts, modeling, rehearsal, and corrective feedback to alter their children's behaviors using contingency management procedures. This guidebook extends these procedures to relatives of older people with behavior problems and teaches caregivers to be more effective in the care they give. Techniques can be used to decrease inappropriate behaviors and to increase desirable behaviors of elderly people and their support persons, thus providing a positive alternative to institutionalization.

LINKAGE WITH COMMUNITY SERVICES

Linking the client to correct available resources in the community is of great concern in social welfare and society at large. This is a particularly important behavioral perspective because such linkage is a major way to increase the client's access to reinforcing consequences that will maintain appropriate behaviors. Assessing the need for and providing appropriate service delivery of community services to the elderly is an ongoing problem that requires the further development and evaluation of procedures. While many referrals for service are made, clients might or might not pursue them. Attempts to obtain service are often discouraged by unreceptive or overworked staff (Kirk & Greenly, 1974), or a mismatch between clients and available resources may occur (Middleman & Goldberg, 1974). Specific methods to monitor linkage activity and resource availability are necessary to provide good service. Although excellent linkage strategies have been delineated by Pincus and Minahan (1973) and Weissman (1976), these linkage methods have not been systematically applied to or rigorously evaluated with the elderly (Middleman & Goldberg, 1974). Weissman (1976) designed a task-centered model of linkage that contained (a) problem identification, (b) resource location, (c) option exploration, (d) resource selection, (e) resource connection, and (f) verification of resource assistance. Other task-centered research and models addressed this problem with other populations (Brown, 1977; Epstein, 1980; Reid, 1978). These problems are central to the maintenance of both elderly persons within the community and their caregivers' support systems.

The family is identified as the major linkage between older people and government bureaucracies. Sussman (1977) viewed the family as a mediating system for elderly people to obtain responsible services from human service organizations. He also stated that the availability of medical care and rehabilitation options for the elderly depends on the financial position of the family; the knowledge, awareness, and motivation of family members including the elderly; and the location of kin, friends, and peer-group members.

Burkhardt (1979) suggested that information and referral aspects of programs provide the basis for service coordination. The process of helping families to develop community service linkages is not a formal part of the service delivery literature, and the methods are not clearly understood. As Frankfather (1977) illustrated, the risk of older persons being caught in the conflict between service programs is a distinct possibility. Community linkages to services are particularly helpful when clients are limited in their ability to seek out resources and to monitor the changing availability of services that meet their needs. This task is compounded by increased psychiatric or physical limitations. An underlying assumption of this program is that support persons can be taught to facilitate the service aspect of intervention and, in some cases, to develop their own community linkages whenever possible.

SUMMARY

Human service professionals assisting older families can draw on a range of research and practice methods in addition to traditional casework and counseling methods. Practitioners can also consider methods being developed that promote family involvement (Sager, 1983). Community service linkages, or case-management methods, although continually recognized as vital in work with older clients, require additional development and backing to become a standard part of home support for the elderly. Finally, a rich practice and research base exists for training families to deal effectively with specific behavior problems. Both the parent-training methods previously tested with children and the behavioral gerontology literature show great promise of being applicable to older families in home settings. Preliminary research conducted by the Elderly Support Project suggests a range of effective interventions to maximize family and community support of the impaired elderly.

Chapter 3
Assessment of Client Problems and Resources

Intervening with problem behaviors of an older person begins with practitioner efforts to understand the behaviors of concern within the environmental and social context. The initial skills to be developed by the professional helper are those necessary for assessment of the client's problems and of the resources available for their solution. Assessment occurs simultaneously with initial client orientation and engagement. Skills necessary to engage the client and the caregiver include provision of clear information about services; adeptness with communication and interviewing methods, particularly with those with sensory impairments; and ability to maximize the reinforcing qualities of home interviews.

This chapter presents assessment methods, including how the practitioner observes, interviews, and administers relevant questionnaires and, together with client and caregiver, delineates target problems, desired outcomes, and ongoing evaluation and measurement strategies. Although the assessment generally starts before formal interventions are introduced, assessment activities are the beginning of active treatment. Assessment continues as part of the intervention and termination phases. Important goals of assessment are to determine whose behavior should change, the relevant behaviors for change, and the environmental events which maintain, discourage, or prevent those behaviors.

An orientation interview with the client and family provides information about the service. The practitioner observes social, memory, and ambulation problems firsthand and estimates the caregiver's motivation to participate in the intervention effort. Assessment continues in a series of home visits by the practitioner, who interviews the client regarding strengths, weaknesses, and previous efforts to solve problems. Direct observations are conducted to inform the practitioner of family interaction patterns, that is, to determine types of initiations and responses that are used. Special attention is focused on what happens before, during, and after behaviors of interest, as well as on alternative behaviors that occur. All unpleasant behaviors do not need to be changed. Rather, focus is on the behaviors or behavioral deficits that are judged most likely to result in transfer of the client to institutional care.

For example, the practitioner noticed that Mr. DeBerry (described in the previous chapter) spent most of his time sitting in a chair or lying in bed while his daughter brought him everything he needed. Their conversation consisted primarily of demands and complaints, with positive statements, questions, or requests. Mr. DeBerry did not ask to be taken to the toilet, and his daughter did not offer him help, although she gave him a great deal of attention after he wet in the chair, much of which was critical of him. The daughter agreed to record a baseline frequency of their conversations, incidents involving memory problems, walking, and toilet use. After one week, the practitioner returned and presented potential suggestions for procedures.

Assessment methods include direct observation of behavior patterns and social initiations and responses, clients' reports of their problems and strengths, and findings from the various questionnaires and scales that provide specific client information. Assessment contributes to a topographical analysis of the baseline findings, in other words, the preintervention patterns of behaviors. This analysis is necessary in order to plan and evaluate structured interventions.

The *functional analysis* of behaviors is "an examination of environmental events that appear to be causally related" to a behavior (Pinkston et al., 1982, p. 20). Functional analysis focuses on components that affect specific behaviors. Within this individualized assessment it is desirable to evaluate consequences and antecedents of behaviors; biological, economic, and social factors; individual abilities; personal history; and relevant group norms (Kanfer & Saslow, 1969).

Three assertions can be supported regarding behavioral excesses and deficits of the elderly:

1. Most behavior problems can be conceptualized as too frequent or infrequent.
2. Problem deficits are frequently associated with absence of adequate positive reinforcers or stimulus cues.
3. Problem excesses are often related to unclear instructions, followed by attention, or they occur when alternative positive behaviors are not reinforced.

Family caregivers easily and frequently identify excessive behaviors such as complaining, smoking, wearing too many clothes, wandering, aggressive speech, crying, or lying in bed. High frequencies of these behaviors are easily conceptualized as excessive. Deficits of behaviors are more difficult because they reflect what is not present, and caregivers possess realistic estimates of the behaviors they would like to see increased. Clients, however, may have better ideas of what they would like to do. When clients and caregivers do not know what behaviors they would like to see increased, some time should be spent with them exploring possible options, that is, assessing their views of positive outcomes to the intervention. A list of events frequently associated with deficits of desired behaviors is generated by the practitioner to suggest possible points of intervention. Among these are

- Physical obstacles to behavior
- Limitations imposed by others
- Limitations imposed by the older person
- Few incentives or worthwhile consequences
- Little or no motivation or suggestions to engage in activity
- Poor physical resources
- Little attention or credit given to the person when behaviors do occur
- Absence of people necessary for behavior to occur

Similarly there are environmental patterns that can be observed when excessive behaviors occur. Among these are

- Inadequate instructions to end behavior
- Few alternative behaviors
- Attention or conversation following the behavior (threats, demands, teasing, or even conversation and praise)
- Anxiety or concern from others

THE BEHAVIORAL PARADIGM

The functional interactions between behaviors and environmental events are called contingencies and include three components: antecedents, behaviors, and consequences.

Antecedent events are any events that occurred prior to the behavior. Antecedents provide a cue that a behavior will or will not occur. These cues help the individual to discriminate when a behavior will be tolerated or when it will render positive outcomes. Because these cues aid in discriminating reinforcement opportunities, they are referred to as discriminative stimuli.

Consequences are the events that occur regularly after a behavior and affect the future probability of occurrence. The effect that consequences have on the future occurrence of a behavior is an essential component in assessing behavior.

In this approach *behaviors* are discussed primarily as the products of antecedent and consequent events, although they are also influenced by the person's genetic endowment, health, and previous experience.

PERSONAL VARIABLES

Assessing a client's skills and health leads to a delineation of positive behaviors to be strengthened and inherent physical limitations requiring compensating environmental conditions, which leads to setting realistic outcomes. No matter how impaired, each client has resources or abilities to contribute to each situation. Practitioners address client strengths first, to help the family choose positive behaviors to build upon as alternatives to behavior deficits. Behavioral intervention with an older client helps that person restore previous skills that have become dormant or that require modification because of physical and social losses or lack of practice or opportunity. It also provides the opportunity to develop and implement programs to increase health-related behaviors. These may include exercise, eating training, or activity programs to insure proper medication practices and so on. Development of health-related behavior is facilitated by cooperation with medical personnel in improving health or increasing understanding of health limitations.

Some inherent limitations, frequently presented by the client's health, may be present initially or may emerge after assessment or intervention begins. In these cases improving alternative coping behaviors is essential. A medical examination is essential to determine the physical costs of efforts to engage in specific activities (see Table 3.1). Even with this information, the actual limits of behavior are not clear until empirical testing of interventions, which is the only way to assess capabilities.

Knowledge of what medications are being used and their possible side effects is important. Many drugs, especially many used by older people, affect behavior and include such side effects as dizziness, disorientation, drowsiness, change in taste reception, and depressive feelings. Also, changes associated with drugs may affect the client's perceptions of available antecedents and consequences. The behavioral data recorded by clients, caregivers, and practitioners can be reported to the medical team to influence their decisions.

At this point in the assessment, the caregiver should be evaluated to determine whether or not he or she is likely to participate successfully in the program, or, if willing, to determine whether he or she has adequate health, time, motivation, and ability. The items on the Caregiver Checklist (Table 3.2) are used more to determine in what areas the caregiver needs

Table 3.1. Referral Procedures

1. Referring staff determines the appropriateness of the client according to the program criteria.
2. Referring staff discusses the program with the client and family. Staff may cover the following points in introducing the program to families:
   A. The project is a family program to teach specific methods to enable older people to live at home.
   B. The program helps the family with specific individual and family problems that occur within the client's home.
   C. Initial contact occurs with program staff.
   D. Distribution and review of brochure.
3. If clients meet the criteria and are interested, referring staff calls the program office to provide a brief description of the family and their needs for service. Information required includes living situation, medical status, diagnosis, medication, other services, and specific problems.
4. Arrangements are made to provide written medical and psychosocial information. Client signs necessary consent forms.
5. Program staff and referring staff determine specific plan to set up initial interview.
6. Program staff assess the appropriateness of the client for the program and inform referring staff of disposition. If subject is not accepted for the program, alternative referrals are made.
7. If subject is accepted for the program, further contact is coordinated by program staff.
8. Program staff report on a quarterly basis to referring staff regarding the status of the case.

Table 3.2. Caregiver Checklist

Worker _____ Date _____

ABILITY

1. Physical health of caregiver:
   —No serious problem
   —Health problems under control
   —Serious but able to function
   —At risk of hospitalization
   —Problems too serious for participation
2. Mental health:
   —No psychological problems
   —Emotionally distressed but no impaired functioning
   —Serious psychological problems but able to function
   —Chronic psychological problems with medication
   —At risk of hospitalization (unworkable)
3. Frequency of contact with client:
   —Lives with
   —Daily
   —Twice weekly (semiweekly)
   —Weekly
   —Monthly
4. Time commitment:
   —Daily
   —Daily phone or twice weekly visit
   —Weekly
   —Monthly
   —Less than monthly

(continued)

Table 3.2. (*continued*)

---

5. Recipient of client's behavior:
   —Daily
   —Daily or biweekly visit
   —Weekly visit
   —Daily phone calls
   —Less than daily phone calls
6. Relationship to client:
   —Sees positive aspects of client
   —Sees some positive qualities with some displeasure
   —Feels obligated to care for client with little positive to say
   —Clearly dislikes client and feels trapped
   —Dislikes client and wants out
7. Motivation of caregiver to participate:
   —Clearly cares for client and feels responsible
   —Sees some positive aspects and feels responsible
   —Feels responsible for family reasons
   —No one else will help
   —Wants someone else to take responsibility but is prevented by financial reasons
8. Control of social consequences:
   —Frequent contact and socially valuable to client
   —Frequent contact but client dislikes
   —Infrequent contact and not valuable to client
   —Too infrequent contact and client does not like
9. Control of material consequences:
   —Frequently provides money and food
   —Provides occasional material treats, food, clothes, activities
   —Provides few extras
   —Provides no extras
   —No ability to provide material comfort
10. Competing demands:
    —None
    —Social activities, or part-time work, or care of other(s)
    —Full-time employment
    —Care of other(s) and employment
    —Extensive care of other(s), distance, and/or employment
11. Ability to record data:
    —Can learn quickly
    —Can learn with practice
    —Would require extensive retraining
    —Cannot follow simple instructions
    —Physically or mentally unable to record or refuses
12. Ability to learn new procedures:
    —Can learn quickly
    —Can learn with practice
    —Would require extensive retraining
    —Cannot follow simple instructions
    —Physically or mentally unable to implement procedures or refuses
13. Attitude toward client's behavior:
    —Realistic view of client's problems
    —Does not understand client's problems
    —Believes incorrectly client's behavior is caregiver's fault
    —Believes incorrectly client is punishing caregiver on purpose
    —Believes incorrectly client is hopeless

(continued)

Table 3.2. (*continued*)

CAREGIVER SUPPORT SYSTEM

14. Help from other family, friends, or neighbors:
    —Daily or more
    —Twice weekly
    —Weekly
    —Biweekly
    —Less than biweekly
15. Help from professional and volunteer organizations:
    —Five days a week or more
    —Two days a week or more
    —Weekly
    —Biweekly
    —Monthly or less
16. Respite care available:
    —Daily or five days a week
    —Two days a week or more
    —Weekly
    —Biweekly
    —Monthly or less
17. Frequency of pleasurable experiences:
    —Daily or more
    —Two or three times a week
    —Weekly
    —Biweekly
    —Monthly or less
18. Frequency of social contacts with family or neighbors:
    —Daily or more
    —Two or three times a week
    —Weekly
    —Biweekly
    —Monthly or less
19. Frequency of social contacts with friends:
    —Two or three times a week
    —Weekly
    —Biweekly
    —Monthly or less
20. Economic resources:
    —Abundant
    —Adequate
    —Limited
    —Inadequate

help and training than to eliminate potential caregivers. If a potential caregiver's score is low on many of the items, the practitioner is cautious in designing the program, to avoid either the client's or caregiver's experiencing failure. Some items suggest that the family member may not be able to conduct the intervention procedures. For instance, risk of mental hospitalization would be an item in this program that would eliminate a person as a candidate for caregiver. It would be poor behavioral programming to add stress to a caregiver who is barely hanging on to his or her mental health. If, for instance, the caregiver is overburdened with the care of others, respite in the form of day care might be sought before a more demanding change procedure was instituted. Slow learning of procedures by the caregiver might be compensated for by breaking procedures into small, incremental steps. The checklist is structured for the practitioner's evaluation of the caregiver's potential, specific strengths, and deficits, rather than for valid measurement purposes.

THE PROSTHETIC ENVIRONMENT

Using a behavioral perspective the practitioner begins with what is directly observable, and then designs changes to create a prosthetic environment. A prosthetic environment (Lindsley, 1964) is one which continues to promote behavior change. This conceptualization differs from the therapeutic environment, in which it is assumed that behavior change will continue after intervention is removed because changes have occurred within the person. Because the emphasis is on antecedents and consequences, it is assumed that they must remain if improved behavior change is to be maintained.

ASSESSMENT COMPONENTS

The formal part of the assessment includes interviews, observations, and completion of questionnaires. Although the structured assessment materials are usually administered to only the client and the caregiver, all family members willing to be involved are interviewed. These relatives may provide information such as social resources for respite care or different perspectives of strengths and problems of the clients and stresses of the caregivers.

Assessment Interviews

Interviews provide opportunities for defining problems in objective terms, assessing resources, setting goals, planning intervention, evaluating progress, and planning the extension of intervention effects (Pinkston et al., 1982). With older clients, sensory abilities and intellectual abilities must be considered. Interviewers should assure clients that they can be heard and understood, by requesting feedback from them intermittently and adjusting their style accordingly. Successful interviews generally include a tone of mutual respect, clear communication of the reasons for questions, and mutual participation by the practitioner and the family. Often clients need signs of understanding, which can be shown through acceptance and positive statements regarding their personal worth (see Table 3.3). Among older clients the mere presence of a person interested in their present, previous, or future life may be perceived as extremely reinforcing or gratifying. Often the opportunity to reminisce, state problems, or discuss future plans is viewed as a positive experience and may be therapeutic. This may be particularly the case with older clients whose physical and social situations have changed so they no longer receive daily recognition or reinforcement of their accomplishments.

The practitioner's first task is to help the client reconceptualize the presenting problems in behavioral terms that facilitate intervention. The practitioner also elicits information from the client through thoughtful questions, which provide data for assessing problems and designing interventions that are likely to help the client avoid negative experiences or obtain more life satisfaction. The practitioner ascertains in early interviews the client's view of a positive outcome (Goldiamond, 1974; Schwartz & Goldiamond, 1975), and what the client says should be different following the intervention. This provides better ideas of what changes need to occur. For example, a family may be referred because of the elderly

Table 3.3. Dos and Don'ts for Interviewing Older Clients

DO . . .
1. Make positive statements, for example, "Nice to see you."
2. Remind client of time and place.
3. Use humor throughout. Laugh with client.
4. Recognize client concerns and complaints. Try to find out more about concerns and restate your understanding.
5. Try to involve client in family interviews by addressing specific questions to him or her.
6. Use questions about the past to help client reminisce, particularly if short-term memory appears to be a problem.
7. Be clear in your plans and commitments. Avoid setting times for interviews that may need to be changed.
8. Plan for subsequent visits, involving client in planning.
9. Try to schedule a regular time for visits and calls.
10. Try to spend time with older client, even if this is limited to sitting, holding hands, and so on.

DON'T . . .
1. Get angry and criticize client for forgetting.
2. Laugh at client's mistakes.
3. Minimize or discourage complaints.
4. Argue with client when he or she blames you or the family for his or her deficits.
5. Make decisions for client when he or she can be involved.
6. Ridicule or minimize client's incapacities.
7. Criticize client's inability to stay in present.
8. Make promises that are not sure of being kept.
9. Change plans frequently without notifying client.
10. Show anger if client spends excessive time complaining.

Note: Adapted from "Backstage at Drexel Home" by Frankel and McCauley, 1977, unpublished manuscript.

mother's hallucinations. Redefining the situation as a positive outcome, the family members may decide that pleasant conversation one half hour per day, continuous sleep 6 hours a night, and an out-of-home activity each day are desired.

It is useful to develop a mechanism for providing positive social consequences for the client. Most often this can take the form of verbal praise and attention, by articulating the strengths of the client that are most likely to be helpful in solving problems or by focusing on the client's attempts to do something about the problems. Positive statements about the client's efforts to obtain assistance direct his or her attention toward strengths and support motivation, increasing the likelihood of desirable change. An older client may have limited social skills, and it may be necessary to pair the practitioner with a material object such as food to strengthen social reinforcement. Giving a ride or going for a walk, sharing a cup of coffee, or listening to music together may facilitate practitioner reinforcement.

For many individuals some specific communication techniques are required. Individualized interview techniques may include touching, increasing response opportunities, summarizing, repeating, and using rest periods. Often shaking hands begins such contact, and holding a client's hand may facilitate attention. Of course touch can be used only when a client appears to initiate or accept such support. A second technique is the pause, or response opportunity. Very often interviewers do not wait long enough for the older person to process questions and communicate answers. Often the client's family answers for them, when, if given time, he or she is able to respond independently. A variation of the pause is repetition. The practitioner can repeat or restate the question or the client's response to improve clarity and allow a longer response opportunity. Frequent summaries of what is planned or what has been achieved in an interview are helpful.

Finally, the older client may have a limited attention span, and rest periods may be needed. The practitioner might ask the client if he or she would like to take a break, might ask for a glass of water, or might simply ask for a few minutes to go over the data collected so far. Helping potential is maximized by the practitioner's ability to focus on the positive aspects of the client and the client's behavior and by insuring that the interview is an occasion for receiving social reinforcement. Some additional interview suggestions are presented in Table 3.3.

In home-based practice, clients include both elderly people and those who provide support for them. Early interviews can be conducted with the family as a whole or with only the target clients and their caregivers. Generally the entire family is interviewed together whenever possible, and questions are directed to the target client first. Often the practitioner asks one family member to ask another a specific question. It is important to remember that practitioners are teaching the family new ways to communicate within the family setting, and, when necessary, to set up the environment to facilitate a successful interview.

Problem Selection

Evaluation of intervention outcomes requires the definition and measurement of relevant intervention and outcome variables. Problem behaviors and desired outcomes are defined in terms of observable responses or events. The assessment in-home interview begins with a discussion of supportive family or concerned friends and environmental resources. These elements help the practitioner to develop a list of potential resources, caregivers or helpers. Questions focus on the older person's strengths and deficits, current behavior, daily activities, and goals for change (Goldiamond, 1974). An initial interview checklist is helpful and provides a series of questions for the assessment phase (see Table 3.4).

The interview is devoted to helping the family define problems in terms of behavioral excesses and deficits. The family then explores specific prob-

Table 3.4. Interview Guide to Assess Problem Behavior

---

1. What are your general concerns right now?
2. What is going well in the situation you are concerned about right now in regard to _____ (the older person)?
   a. How does _____ contribute to the family?
   b. What things can _____ do for himself or herself? What strengths are present?
   c. What things should not change?
   d. Are there some additional areas that should change besides the behaviors you have described?
3. I am now going to ask some questions to help us both better understand what we should work toward.
   a. If we were totally successful what would be the result for your family?
   b. Exactly what would change, and how would things be different?
   c. How is this different from what is happening now?
4. Can you describe the problem behavior(s) in more detail?
   a. When do they occur? (times)
   b. How often do they occur?
   c. What things occur prior to the behavior? (Antecedents)
   d. How long has this been happening?
   e. Are there situations or conditions when the present behavior occurs but is not a problem?
   f. How have you dealt with the problem in the past? Is this successful?
   g. Who helps with the problem? Is there any one person who deals with it more successfully than others?
   h. Why is this a problem that needs to be solved right now?
5. What are the consequences of this behavior?
   a. Has the older person been excused from things that might not otherwise occur?
   b. How do people respond when the behavior occurs? Is the person given or denied special attention because of the behavior?

---

lems and their expectations for change. Components of the specific problem are explored, with the family trying to determine possible antecedents and consequences of the behavior. A fine-grained analysis of the problem begins with asking the family questions on specific areas, such as why the problem is of special urgency now, how the problem specifically interferes with the daily life of the older person, alternative behaviors that the older person engages in, and potential obstacles to change. If additional problems exist, the practitioner repeats the process with each problem.

The practitioner, the older person, and the caregivers describe in specific terms the situations in which behaviors occur, define behavioral and environmental events, and select methods to record behaviors. The considerations in problem selection are expressed in terms of client desire, educational potential, potential for problem alleviation, and maintenance of change. The goal of problem exploration is to select the one to three behaviors that are of greatest concern to the client and the family.

Observations

Following the definition of specific targets or goals, the practitioner teaches the older person, relatives, and significant others basic data-recording procedures to be used at home. This is a distinctive feature of behavioral treatment. Although other approaches have provided careful assessment of family counseling to older families, few have operationalized behaviors as intervention targets, carefully measuring the occurrence of these behaviors across the duration of the treatment, and used these measures as clinical material for the formulation and evaluation of treatment.

Very often an observation session follows the initial interview. During this session the practitioner spends an hour or more at the client's home, observing interactions and activities. When possible, another observer besides the practitioner participates. From these observations a pattern of client behavior and environmental events emerges that helps to define appropriate and inappropriate behaviors for more careful observations and for later intervention. *Anecdotal observations* are usually recorded in three columns: antecedent events, client behaviors, and consequent events, with all client behaviors being recorded in the center column. The arrangement provides the groundwork for a preliminary functional analysis of the client's interaction with the environment and a more accurate guess at appropriate and inappropriate behaviors to be measured. Thus behaviors of others in the client's environment, as well as the client's behaviors, are included.

An example of this observational assessment is illustrated in Table 3.5. Mr. Young was referred to a home health care social worker because the

Table 3.5. Anecdotal Record

Antecedent	Client Behavior	Consequences
	5:15 p.m. Watching television sitting on couch.	
Grandson enters room and asks Mr. Y. how he is doing.	Mumbles.	Grandson asks question.
Grandson asks another question.	Answers briefly. Looks at grandson very briefly, then looks at television.	Grandson leaves room.
Wife asks about checks from other room.	Responds "Yeah."	Wife enters room with checks to be signed.
Wife asks him to sign checks.	Signs check.	Wife asks him to sign second check.
Wife asks him to sign second check.	Signs second check.	
Wife asks him about not feeling well.	No response.	Wife asks him to sign third check.
Wife asks him to sign third check.	Signs third check.	Wife compliments him on signatures.
Wife asks two questions.	Says "no" to both.	Wife leaves room.
Wife leaves room.	Watches television.	
Wife says "You did not eat the cauliflower."	Says: "I didn't know how to fix it."	Wife explains how to cook cauliflower.
Wife explains how to cook cauliflower.	No response.	

This record elicits data on the behavior of the older client and on the antecedent and consequential behaviors by support persons. For each behavior observed in the subject, a brief description is recorded in the client column, and the prior activities and consequent responses are recorded in the other columns.

family and the home care nurse were concerned about his low activity level, his refusal to converse or socialize, and his general depression. His severe cardiac condition placed some limitations on active behaviors. During a preliminary anecdotal observation (Table 3.5), the practitioner found that Mr. Young was not responsive to efforts by family members to converse with him (he mumbled or answered in very brief sentences). The practitioner also observed that family members had the required prompting and praising abilities to elicit behaviors and that Mr. Young's activities were indeed very low level and nonsocial in form. The assessment helped the practitioner and the family select some target behaviors for further assessment and intervention: positive statements by Mr. Young, responses of more than three words, praise by family members, and increasing out-of-home activities.

Anecdotal observations take place at times when problematic behaviors are most likely to occur. For example, Mrs. Randolph requested help in supporting her mother, who lives with her. She reported that her mother argued constantly, and in a very critical manner, with her two grandchildren. The practitioner asked when this particular difficulty tended to occur. Mrs. Randolph stated that mealtimes were the most argumentative time. A mealtime observation was then set up as the next contact.

The most accurate source of data for evaluation is direct observation (Baer, Wolf, & Risley, 1968; Bijou, Peterson, & Ault, 1968; Hersen & Barlow, 1976). Direct observation refers to systematic viewing of relevant behaviors (Pinkston et al., 1982). The observer—either caregiver, practitioner, or other family member—watches the way the client interacts with people and objects in the environment to note the occurrence of the identified behavior and records it at specified time periods, either within a time interval or at the end of a time sample.

Why are direct observations important? Direct observations provide a permanent record of the frequency of the problem behavior. After recording this information the family and the practitioner can decide together if the suspected problem indeed occurred at problematic levels and how it changes over time. The following steps are used to develop observation codes:

- Identify behaviors to be observed.
- Define behaviors in highly specific terms.
- Select an observer who has the skills to learn to observe, who is present when the problem or desired activity occurs, who wants to help, and who is willing to record on a daily basis. The observer may be the client or the major caregiver. Practitioners or special observers may, however, observe and compile data. For example, the clients could turn on a tape recorder to record conversations so that the practitioner can code the tapes later.
- Determine when observations will occur. Observation times must be convenient for observers and those at home and reflect usual behavior patterns during problem times.
- Provide a recording instrument. This can be a checklist, a card for tally work, a specific data collection form, or a log or diary.
- Develop recording instructions that are presented in written and oral format to all related family members.
- Help the client practice recording by demonstrating procedures, encouraging practice, and giving corrective feedback.

- Observe simultaneously with family observers to determine accuracy or reliability.
- Establish an observation schedule agreement.

Problem and desired behaviors are measured in terms of frequency, duration, latency, and intensity. Frequency and duration are the most useful in practice because they are simple and more reliably measured. The client or caregiver records, usually within a specific time period, each occurrence of the behavior. Mrs. Kent, for example, was very concerned that her husband spent so much time in bed. A simple checklist was developed that she could use to check if the client was out of bed for the entire hour. Hours in which the client spent any time in bed were not counted toward the total time out of bed. Frequency of smoking, activities in and out of the home, and visitors were also recorded (see Figure 3.1 for example of form).

When asking the caregiver or client to record frequency or duration, the recording method should be kept simple, indicating how often the behavior occurs; how long it lasts; how long between occurrences of the behavior; how intense it is; and how loud or assertive the client is.

Because interventions are designed to alter the consequences following behavior, these consequences should be defined and measured along with client behaviors. If an intervention is planned, the elements of that intervention should be coded and measured. The young woman who plans to increase her assertiveness with her mother will need to record her assertive statements as well as her mother's responses to these statements.

The family, the older client, and the practitioner provide a base through which *interobserver reliability* is collected. Once successful, baseline data are collected by the family for at least one week, with reliability recorded at least once with an observer. With five to seven data points, the family can determine the overall frequency, stability of baseline behavior, consequences, antecedents, and other data from which to proceed in the intervention training.

Reliability is a scientific term that refers to methods that ascertain whether reported client information is accurate. By having an additional observer record data simultaneously with the regular recorder, the results can be compared to determine the degree of accuracy of observations. This is important in all assessment and research, but particularly important when the recorder is the client or the caregiver, who may have a specific interest in reflecting particular trends in behavior. Often clients and caregivers wish to please practitioners or wish behaviors to appear worse than they actually are. The simplest way to avoid these problems is to schedule regular checks of recording accuracy. Results of simultaneous observations

FIGURE 3.1. Activity record

Date _____ Name _____

Please check when behaviors occur each hour. Fill out a new sheet each day.

TIME	Smoking	In Bed	Out of House	Telephone	Visitor	TV	Other
7–8 a.m.							
8–9 a.m.							
9–10 a.m.							
10–11 a.m.							
11–12 a.m.							
12–1 p.m.							
1–2 p.m.							
2–3 p.m.							
3–4 p.m.							
4–5 p.m.							
5–6 p.m.							
6–7 p.m.							
7–8 p.m.							
8–9 p.m.							
9–10 p.m.							
10–11 p.m.							
11–12 p.m.							
12–7 a.m.							

can be assessed by comparing the percentage of agreement on times that each behavior has occurred during each interval. A simple formula for computing reliability scores divides the instances of agreement that a behavior has occurred by the instances of agreement plus disagreement that a behavior has occurred and then multiplies the result by 100% $\{[\text{agreement}/(\text{agreement} + \text{disagreement})] \times 100\%\}$. In general, when the percentage of agreement is above 80%–85%, acceptable reliability can be concluded. With very low frequency behaviors, percentage of agreement that the behavior did not occur may be substituted for percentages of agreement that the behavior did occur, using the same formula.

For example, Mr. Green and his daughter have agreed to participate in the behavioral program. The focus of the data collection and intervention will be verbal communications, which are suspected to occur at low rates. A practitioner trains the family in the use of the Family Behavior Record (see Figure 3.2). The problem behavior (low rates of verbal conversation) has been operationalized. The practitioner then trains Mr. Green and his daughter in the exact steps for recording the behavior and practices, using the Family Behavior Record. A tape recording of a simulated interaction is used as the basis of training. Training continues with the family until an 80% reliability score is obtained. The practitioner then shifts from the simulated tape to actual in-home observations. Predefined observational techniques are used. The observer continues the training until high reliability is obtained from the in-home observation.

As the initial information-gathering phase is completed, the practitioner reviews behavioral goals with each family member, insuring that each understands the need for behavioral change. The practitioner's goal now is to interpret the program to all family members with sufficient clarity and specificity that each relevant person fully understands its goals and his or her part in achieving those goals. Special efforts are made to engage several family members and other supporters in the treatment process, to determine their reservations about the program and procedures, and to respond to such reservations in order to establish a mutually acceptable working agreement that will maintain the client and his or her engagement.

INDIRECT MEASURES

Although direct observation and self-observation are the most important direct measures of behavioral variables, other types of information are used in the assessment of the client and the evaluation of direct interventions. Less direct sources of information can be used to provide additional information regarding the effectiveness of assessment and intervention, especially to tap personality, attitudinal, health, and intellectual

FIGURE 3.2. Family behavior record

Name: Mr. Green   Date: Wednesday, November 3

Behavior: Conversation—*Communication or talking where Mr. G says at least three words in response to questions or statements by another family member.*

Please note when the behavior occurs before and after.

TIME		BEFORE	DURING	Describe what others did AFTER the behavior occurred. Check box.					
start	stop	What happened before the behavior occurred?	What happened when the behavior occurred?	Did not notice	Ignored	Criticized	Asked to do something else	Praised or rewarded	Other
9:00	9:03	Sitting at table	Asked for more breakfast					x	Gave more eggs
9:05	9:07	Asked what will do today	Said he would like to go for walk					x	
10:30	10:33	Returned from walk	Complained about cold				x		
TOTAL			3				1	2	

dimensions. For proper application of behavioral procedures, practitioners must also be scientists who are interested in how these components of the clients' lives change as behavioral training is introduced. Questionnaires are administered during the initial contact phase as a pretest and at least once more, often near termination, as a posttest. Whenever possible, more frequent application provides more believable and valid information, which can be correlated with recordings of interim interventions and changes in life events.

The Elderly Support Project preassessment package includes two major questionnaires: The Older Person Pretest Questionnaire (OPPQ) and the Relative Pretest Questionnaire (RPQ). The purpose of the preassessments is to allow the practitioner to make accurate assessments concerning the ability and disability of the clients in major areas of their lives. These questionnaires incorporate components of a number of standardized instruments. They are adapted from the Older Americans Resource and Services Program (OARS) multi-dimensional assessment (Pfeiffer, 1978), with several additions.

The pre-post assessment includes

- The Adult Personality Rating Scale (Kleban, Brody, & Lawton, 1971), in which family members rate older relatives on many variables
- The Family Burden Scale (Zarit, Reever, & Bachman Peterson, 1980), which measures the perceived burden of caregivers
- Mental Status (R. L. Kahn, Goldfarb, Pollack, & Peck, 1960) and Face-Hand tests (Bender, Fink, & Green, 1951), which assess orientation
- A simple hearing test, using a telephone message provided by the local hearing society
- Client specification of social resources, including perceived families, friends, and the frequency of their contacts with each other
- Client and caregiver estimates of economic resources
- Client and caregiver assessment of mental health and completion by client of a mental health rating scale (Pfeiffer, 1978)
- Estimates of physical health problems and health resources used and completion of a checklist of health problems and medications used
- Use of supportive devices
- Activity of Daily Living assessments (Sources: Pfeiffer, 1978; Shanas, 1962)
- Assessment of social activities both at home and out of home (includes current and desired frequency and opinions of what may change other than frequency)
- Delineation of four target behavior problems and estimates of their seriousness (completed by client, caregiver, and practitioner)
- Specification of caregiving provided by caregiver and others

- Specification of participation in community services
- Caregiver rating of own abilities to manage behavior problems[1]

These assessment methods provide a variety of data for formulating interventions. Client self-reports through initial interviews give the client and the caregiver perceptions of problems and strengths and provide clues as to additional intervention resources. This information may be further supplemented by client and caregiver completion of questionnaires that provide more specific data in standardized form. Although such standardization is still in the elementary stages, over time the practitioner will learn to make decisions about treatment from initial levels of activities and attitudes reported on such questionnaires. Practitioner observations also add informal information and structured information to the assessment. Finally, client observations and caregiver observations give daily frequencies of target behavior levels. What emerges from the assessment is a functional analysis of the behaviors. The frequency of behaviors and the related antecedents, consequences, and personal strengths and limitations help the practitioner and the family to select intervention goals, to select target behaviors, and to eventually evaluate change outcomes.

[1]Samples of these questionnaires are available from the authors.

Chapter 4
Intervention Procedures and Guidelines

Assisting family members and elderly clients to alter problem interactions, to provide tangible and needed services, and to increase the occasions and opportunities for stimulation are the goals of any intervention promoting change or maintenance of change. Home-based behavioral interventions build upon an existing and tested model of family intervention and adapt the model's various components to the needs, abilities, and disabilities of an elderly population. As with most structured efforts to modify behavior, this program establishes its particular components according to the individual characteristics of each client, the people that the client interacts with, and the environmental contingencies. It provides realistic and important documentation as different problems are modified, diverse techniques are attempted, and the successes and failures of those efforts are revealed.

Assessment accomplishes a number of tasks: a thorough familiarization with the general circumstances surrounding the identified client, a specification of target problems and their relative importance, a contingency analysis depicting the antecedents and consequences of those target problems, and daily observations by trained family members or other observers. After assessment, emphasis is shifted from gathering information to using that information to formulate and implement efficient and effective behavioral interventions.

Contacts with family members have centered on the practitioner's gathering information and using it to formulate ideas about possible interventions. The information collected during the assessment is used to teach family members new methods of interacting with the client that produce meaningful and socially relevant change.

33

THE CAREGIVER

Behavioral interventions require a person at home who assumes responsibility for using the behavioral techniques the practitioner teaches. This person is referred to as the caregiver. The practitioner teaches the agent of change to alter his or her own behavior or to reorganize household tasks and other schedules to reduce the problem behavior of the identified client.

The practitioner is not the ideal person to be the caregiver because of his or her limited interaction with the client. A 2-hour interview represents less than 3% of the time the client spends each week with family members, friends, and professionals. Employing this support network to the fullest possible extent, therefore, increases vastly the opportunities to modify the client's behavior. The caregiver is selected from family members and friends and taught requisite skills. The tasks of the caregiver are detailed elsewhere (Fischer & Gochros, 1975; Green, 1982; Pinkston et al., 1983), but they include consistently using the techniques developed, reporting difficulties, noting successes, providing reinforcement opportunities, and assisting the practitioner in problem assessment.

Guidelines for selecting caregivers for older people have not been clearly tested. The caregiver must be someone who has important interactions with the elderly client and who is willing to assume the tasks of the change agent. The caregiver checklist (Table 3.2) may be useful in evaluating potential caregivers. Choice in selecting the caregiver is often limited. Most likely, the caregiver will be the spouse, if the client is married to a capable person. Otherwise the caregiver is likely to be a friend or one of the client's children. Although one person will usually serve as the main caregiver, attempts should be made to involve as many of the people who regularly interact with the client as possible in the overall change effort.

Excellent opportunities to describe the probable course of the intervention arise in the process of selecting the change agent. In describing the tasks of the caregiver, typical situations and anecdotes from previous cases can be included. The practitioner can reemphasize the fact that the caregiver will be making systematic changes in his or her own behavior to affect the behaviors of the client. Finally, the selection of a caregiver allows the family members reasonable opportunities to withdraw from the intervention if they decide that the tasks involved are too much for them to undertake at the time. It also allows practitioners to negotiate reasonable alternatives to the required tasks with family members.

It is advantageous to consider using the person trained to be the observer, if a family member, as the caregiver. Many of the traits that make for excellent observers also make for excellent caregivers. Among them are the ability to discriminate the occurrence and nonoccurrence of a target behavior, the ability to engage in a task contingent on the occurrence of the behavior (act or record), and the necessary time and commitment. Although the roles of caregiver and observer are different, many of the necessary skills overlap and complement each other.

GOALS

The practitioner, after a thorough and complete assessment and the collection of baseline data, develops with the client, family members, institutional staff personnel, and other significant individuals a comprehensive statement of the desired effects of intervention, or how things will be different after successful treatment. The practitioner assists the clients, the caregiver, and significant others in the development of time-limited, achievable goals. This process is begun by eliciting from the family members and the client their perceptions of the current problems including their frequency and typical family responses to them. From this summary, the practitioner presents detailed information on what will be different following intervention. An increase in self-care skills as a goal, for instance, is inadequate. The practitioner can use this general and vague goal to define explicit behavioral goals. Components of appropriate goals include (a) the exact nature of the problem, (b) how the problem will be different as a result of treatment, (c) where that change will occur, and (d) whose behavior will change.

The development of goals necessitates the involvement of significant others including the caregiver and service providers. Because of the unique nature of the interactions between a client and significant family members, a common statement of goals must often be negotiated. It is important to spend the time and effort before intervention to develop an agreed-upon common statement of goals. This avoids the possibility of involving an individual with the potential for sabotaging successful behavior change.

Goals for an impaired elderly person are highly individualized. They are directly related to the target problem and should be formulated in concise, short, specific statements. In the process of generating goals, the practitioner should attempt to involve the client. If the client has intellectual limitations, the practitioner should explain the goals in simple and understandable terms and attempt to get the client to restate them in his or her own words, to increase identification and agreement with the goals.

BEHAVIOR CHANGE STRATEGIES

The practitioner begins each program design by using the functional analysis presented earlier, the observational data, and the anecdotal reports, selecting from one of three directions that guide intervention efforts. If the data reveal overt deficiencies in behaviors, a behavioral program is developed that increases opportunities for stimulation and reinforcement or increases contingent reinforcement. If data reveal an excess in behavioral frequency, efforts are directed toward reducing those excessive behaviors while increasing positive adaptive behaviors that are incompatible with the undesired activities.

Increasing Opportunities for Reinforcement

Practitioner efforts attempt to increase the frequency and quality of opportunities for reinforcement. Reinforcement is a primary focus when assessment and baseline information reveal that contingent family responses are given for appropriate behaviors but that there are barriers or other stimuli that interfere with opportunities for the client to engage in reinforcing behaviors. Opportunities to engage in behavior are lost when others take over many of the day-to-day tasks the client formerly engaged in, often as a result of the client's illness. For example, an elderly client who lives alone may never relearn to shop for groceries following recovery from a stroke because the daughter has taken over this task. A client may never have an opportunity to cook again because family members removed the gas control on the stove after the client was burnt once. Limitations on opportunities for reinforcement often result from the reactions of family members to a previous problem situation. Family members remove the responsibility for specific behaviors, and the concomitant opportunity to receive reinforcement through their successful performance, because of past client failures to adequately perform the task.

Family members are not the only individuals with the power to remove or limit behavioral opportunities for reinforcement. Medical personnel frequently make recommendations that inadvertently limit behavioral opportunities. A physician may recommend that an ambulatory patient be restricted to a wheelchair because of falling incidents. Once in the wheelchair, the client can never be reinforced for attempting to walk even though the physiological ability exists. Or, a physician may prescribe major tranquilizers because of overt displays of verbal aggression. The medication effectively reduces the verbal aggression, but it also reduces the overall level of verbalizations, thereby reducing opportunities for the client to be reinforced for appropriate verbal behaviors. Other examples are elderly clients who refuse to leave home because of fear of crime. Staying inside effectively eliminates major opportunities for interpersonal socializing.

Intervention strategies develop programs that teach family members to *increase the naturally occurring cues and prompts* in the home environment. Ogden Lindsley (1964) was among the first to propose that increasing these cues is an effective technique for expanding the opportunities for, and thus the reinforcement of, deficit behaviors. The practitioner teaches family members to set the client up for reinforcement and to assure that the client is reinforced for the target behavior. These behavioral programs necessitate that the client have the physiological abilities and skills to perform the behavior and that, if the behavior were to occur, it would normally be reinforced.

The environmental cues taught to family members do not have to be complex. Linsk taught a social worker in a reorientation group for impaired elderly clients simply to ask more questions (Linsk, Howe, & Pinkston, 1975). This research demonstrated that increasing questions resulted in more task-oriented verbalizations by the elderly clients. Blackman (1981) has shown that asking clients to dress increases those clients' independent dressing abilities. Blackman's research is important because the staff in the residential facility where the study was undertaken indicated that the clients involved did not have the ability to dress themselves. These studies point to the promising ability that simple cues, questions, and requests all have in increasing environmental opportunities and subsequent reinforcement of target behaviors.

Socialization deficits of the impaired elderly are frequently targets for change. Clients often lack social contacts because there is no one to interact with at home, because family members find those interactions punishing, because clients fear leaving the home, or because clients experience mobility difficulties. Increasing the opportunities for reinforcement is a viable method of increasing socialization. Depending on the level of impairment, suitable services are often available in the community. These services include nutrition sites, meals-on-wheels programs, adult day treatment, in-home housekeeping or nursing care, and respite care. As Weissman has illustrated (1976), arranging these services is more complex than just giving the family the name and phone number of a service agency. It is typical for practitioners to arrange transportation, find the closest or most appropriate service, handle financial agreements with service providers, quell family fears, and educate service providers on behavioral techniques appropriate to their relationship with the client.

Teaching family members to use environmental cues and community or home-help services has two functions. One is to increase the opportunities for client reinforcement. The second is to reduce the amount of care family members need to provide. As clients become more impaired, the stress increases for family members. Family members often find their own lives restricted because of their caretaking responsibilities. Clients who increase skills and behaviors that are deficient are likely to reduce the quality and quantity of needed care provided by relatives. Increasing environmental opportunities provides clients and their family members with increased opportunities to engage in reinforcing activities.

Increasing Behaviors

Deficit behaviors are targeted for increase when caregivers learn to use contingent reinforcement techniques to increase the frequency or duration of low-frequency behaviors. Among the techniques family members can be taught to use are more frequent praise, social attention, touch, special activities, enjoyable activities, and tangible reinforcers like food, cigarettes, or physical stimulation.

Practitioners should avoid complex reinforcers when possible. The elderly are frequently in such a state of deprivation that simple reinforcers like touch and attention are sufficiently powerful to accomplish desired changes. It is impossible for practitioners to know in advance which reward will actually reinforce and increase a desired behavior. Attention may be reinforcing to one client but not to another. Only a functional analysis can establish a reward as a reinforcer. Guidelines for selecting potential reinforcers are (a) to select those activities that are already enjoyed and that occur naturally, (b) to select simple reinforcers such as touch, smiles, and attention, (c) to select reinforcers that are compatible with the family values, and (d) to avoid tangible reinforcers when possible.

The contingency analysis is used to determine reinforcers with a potential for increasing a deficit behavior. What can maintain one behavior can frequently be used to increase another. In addition, to reinforce a deficit behavior, practitioners can select an activity or behavior that occurs frequently (Premack, 1959). A client who often telephones, for example, can be asked to keep the activity of telephoning contingent upon the occurrence of a target deficit behavior. Cleaning can be made contingent upon daily walks. Smoking cigarettes can be made contingent upon out-of-bed activities.

Once the practitioner and the client select a behavior or activity for use as a reinforcer, it should be ascertained whether the activity or behavior can be used contingently. Change agents and clients often resist using certain activities contingently, and, if this occurs, the practitioner should select an alternative activity. Asking family members and the client if they can use the activity or behavior as a contingent reinforcer is essential.

Deficit behaviors often have to be broken down into simple components. The desired behavior is broken into its successive tasks. Dressing is a complex task involving numerous skills and components. Skills include gross- and fine-motor coordination, eye-hand coordination, ability to discriminate shapes and colors, and grasping abilities. Components of washing a dish, for example, include scraping excess food into the garbage, filling the sink with hot water, soaking the dish in the hot water, washing the dish with a dishcloth, rinsing the dish with clean water, placing the dish in a dish rack, drying the dish, and placing the dish in the cupboard. Each component is a step toward the completion of the task. Self-care skills with impaired elderly clients can be successfully increased when the behavior is broken down into its simple parts and contingent reinforcement is given for successful performance of each step.

When the physiological impairment is severe, practitioners should develop alternative behaviors for reinforcement. If an increase in dressing is the target behavior, loafers might be substituted for shoes that tie. Pullover shirts can be substituted for shirts that button. The practitioner then shifts to training the caregiver to increase the overall behavior rather than attempting to increase components of the behaviors.

Once the appropriate behavior is targeted and the potential reinforcers are established, the practitioner teaches the caregiver to use the reinforcer contingent on the occurrence of the desired behavior. Family members are taught basic guidelines of reinforcement: that it be given after the behavior has occurred, given immediately by the caregiver, *accompanied* by social and physical attention, and given in a *positive manner*.

The use of contingent reinforcement by caregivers is a simple procedure, although effective use may require focused training and practice. Initial attempts of caregivers to alter their responses to a specified behavior are often uneven. It is frequently quite hard not to lapse into the prior behavioral pattern that maintained the undesired behaviors. Old behavior patterns are formed from persistent habits, and alternative habits must be taught and conscientiously practiced. The practitioner assures adequate use of contingent reinforcement by monitoring data reports, using reliability checks, and providing initial and subsequent instructions. The practitioner uses caregivers' actual performances as analytic tools to determine the successful use of interventions, rather than accepting verbal descriptions of performance.

Increasing contingent reinforcement has two purposes. One is to increase the frequency of positive behaviors through the caregiver's contingent praise, touch, social attention, or tangible rewards. A second purpose is to increase the overall amount of stimulation available to the client at home. Impaired elderly people, because of their physical disabilities or dependence on others, are often deprived of social excitement or physical contact. They may not talk to anyone for hours and enjoy only minimal tactile stimulation or physical affection. The only social stimulation may be the television. To increase the physical, verbal, and auditory stimulation of a deprived individual is often a major intervention objective.

Decreasing Behaviors

Family members frequently cite negative behaviors as their primary concern regarding an aging relative. The client cries too much, is too dependent on others for assistance, doesn't use the toilet, or doesn't leave home.

These negative behaviors are appropriate for behavioral programming efforts.

The goal of any behavioral program is to maximize reinforcing opportunities. Punishment procedures that diminish reinforcement, either through the presentation of an aversive stimulus or the removal of a reinforcer, are avoided. Programming goals are to decrease the excessive behavior while increasing a positive adaptive, yet incompatible, behavior. Incompatible behaviors are behaviors and activities that cannot occur at the same time as target negative behavior. Pleasant talk and accusations are incompatible because it is impossible for both to occur simultaneously. Programming efforts are devoted to increasing social activities, as opposed to reducing isolation. If out-of-home activity increases, excessive time in bed will be reduced.

This technique, *increasing incompatible behaviors,* is often the initial programming effort. Practitioners teach the family caregiver to use reinforcement, or shaping, to increase incompatible behavior. Selecting the incompatible counterpart of a negative behavior is a difficult but creative task for the practitioner. First, the practitioner develops lists of behaviors targeted for increase that, by their occurrence, prevent problem behavior from occurring. The practitioner then teaches the family caregiver to reinforce a positive component of the target behavior which needs strengthening. Every behavior can be stated as an excess or deficit. When stated as a deficit, this component of the behavior is the target for increase. Instead of programming for a decrease in sloppy eating, a more appropriate method is to program for an increase in the deficit positive component— neat dining habits.

A client who complains about tension, nervousness, and anxiety may find relaxation training a helpful incompatible behavior. A structured procedure, often recorded on an audiotape, may direct the client to relax and tense specific muscles or breathe in a systematic way. The client is given a tape recorder and asked to listen to the tape and practice relaxing once or twice a day. In a later phase, the client may be taught to pair the exercise with a specific situation. Finally, the client may be instructed to use the procedure independently, without the tape. The procedure has been used with identified clients as well as support people.

Family members, when presented with these positive intervention strategies, often assert that the primary problem is being avoided. Practitioners should explain the connection between the deficit and the excess behaviors and the fact that the frequency, duration, or intensity of the negative behavior will be decreased as a consequence of promoting positive behaviors. They should then explain the connection between increasing positive behaviors and eliminating problem behaviors. Occasionally caregivers should be told that aversive or punishment techniques may be harmful, ineffective, or even likely to increase the negative behavior.

Difficulties may arise with reinforcing incompatible behaviors. If those difficulties continue or the technique is ineffective, the practitioner can teach an alternative intervention technique. This technique, *differential attention,* reinforces the positive component of a behavior while systematically ignoring the negative component of the behavior. Differential attention has received mixed evaluations of effectiveness (Herbert et al., 1973; Wahler, 1969), but initial reports suggest that it may be a powerful tool with older families (Green, Linsk, & Pinkston, 1980).

Family members are taught to ignore constant nagging by an older relative *and* reinforce pleasant conversations, or to ignore repetitive actions *and* reinforce the single performance of a positive behavior. It is critical to teach family members that the reinforcement component of the technique is as important as the ignoring component and that ignoring is never used alone.

Differential attention gives the family caregiver something to do when negative components of the behaviors occur: Ignore the behavior. Structured methods and monitoring procedures are available to assist in avoiding overuse of ignoring. The frequency of ignoring can be monitored by attending to the data recorded by the client. Excessive ignoring is usually indicated by an overall decrease in the client's positive behaviors. If this occurs the practitioner helps the family increase the positive reinforcers associated with positive behaviors or increase cues to signal the desirability of positive activity. By the use of strong reinforcement techniques, contingent and effective reinforcers, and detailed guidelines for using these procedures, the practitioner is able to effectively teach the family caregiver what to do to improve behaviors, as opposed to paying undue attention to the client's negative behaviors.

Table 4.1 presents a summary of intervention techniques. These are taught to caregivers, emphasizing the behavioral conditions surrounding the problem and family responses to the problem. Practitioners frequently intervene relative to more than one problem and teach family members more than one of the behavioral techniques.

TRAINING AND DELIVERY SYSTEMS

Training family caregivers to contingently alter their responses to their relatives' target requires a structured educational approach. The goal of this training is to teach caregivers the skills and knowledge necessary to use the technique independently of the practitioner, practitioner feedback, and clinical sessions. Delivery systems, contingency contracts, individualized attention programs, and token economies supplement practitioner efforts in training family caregivers to alter their contingent responses.

Table 4.1. Intervention Selection Guidelines

ASSESSMENT	INTERVENTION
Behaviors do not occur at all.	Modeling cues or instructions are the interventions of choice.
Behaviors occur but are very weak, infrequent, or not followed by reinforcing consequences.	Shaping (reinforcement of successive approximations); reinforcement may be increased or introduced.
Behaviors occur but not consistently or at the proper time.	Additional prompts, cues, or schedules. Contracting.
Behaviors occur excessively, or frequently occur when it is undesirable.	Avoidance of reinforcement of the behaviors; differential attention; removal of individual to an environment where behaviors will not be reinforced. Reinforcement of incompatible behaviors.
Behaviors occur that are dangerous to individual or others.	Removal of person from reinforcing environment. Prompting of desirable behavior.
Alternative behaviors limit positive behaviors (pacing, "nervous behaviors," crying).	Introduction of activites incompatible with undesired response, positive relaxation, and so on.

Educating the Caregiver

A didactic approach is used to teach a change agent the behavioral techniques. The practitioner first presents each technique verbally. The practitioner describes the technique, when it is used, and when it is not used. For instance, the practitioner tells the family caregiver to touch the elderly relative every time the relative uses the bathroom independently. The particulars of touching are described. Explanations of when *not* to touch the relative, when assistance is unnecessary, are also included in the description.

Informing a caregiver of how to perform a behavioral technique is often insufficient. The change agents might not understand the technique and its uses and timing, or might state that he or she can perform the technique, when, in reality, he or she cannot. It is advantageous to accompany verbal descriptions with demonstrations and role plays. The technique is demonstrated or modeled for the caregiver by the practitioner. The practitioner's modeling of the technique demonstrates to the caregiver how and when to use the technique and also demonstrates to the client that target behaviors will be reinforced. After the practitioner has modeled the technique for the family caregiver, the practitioner has the caregiver demonstrate the technique in role plays. This demonstration by the caregiver can use either real situations that arise in the clinical interviews or hypothetical situations.

These demonstrations by the caregiver provide the practitioner with opportunities to offer feedback and reinforcement for the correct use of the technique. If difficulties arise, the practitioner can cue the family when to use the technique. This might include spending time at the home of the elderly client specifically to monitor and cue the change agent when to use the technique.

Training of caregivers then shifts focus from in-session training of caregivers to outside-of-session performance of the behavioral technique. This shift occurs only after the family caregivers have successfully demonstrated the technique in session. Once caregivers use the technique outside of the sessions, the practitioner should observe family interactions, alone or with a trained observer, to assure accurate use of the technique. If difficulties arise, these problems can be ameliorated in the clinical sessions.

The absolute effectiveness of different training components, of course, will not be demonstrated until desired behavior changes can be documented. However, using a variety of techniques, assuring that they are individualized for a family, and providing frequent and contingent reinforcement and feedback make it likely that the caregiver will use the developed technique correctly in day-to-day interactions with the client.

Delivery Systems

If problems arise when the caregiver implements the behavioral techniques or if the practitioner believes that the caregiver's ability to alter contingent responses is limited, the practitioner can structure the intervention technique through several methods including contingency contracts, individualized programs, and token economies. *Contingency contracts* include a specification of what reinforcer will be provided when a particular behavior occurs. Contracts are feasible with the elderly provided they have the capacity to negotiate the provisions. Dimensions relevant to contracts are the provisions for the "if . . . then" relationship. *If* a client takes a daily walk, *then* a specific consequence, a special dessert, is provided. Among the problems altered by use of contracts are phobias, low-rate social interactions, high-rate complaining, cigarette use, excessive amounts of time in bed. When the elderly person is involved in the negotiation of the terms of the contracts, the caregiver is often reminded by the elderly relative to deliver agreed-upon reinforcers. This involvement of the client serves to give feedback to the caregiver that the negotiated terms have been met.

An individualized *attention and feedback program* is developed to increase the frequency of contingent reinforcement provided by the caregiver. Practitioners often find that the caregiver has the skills and knowledge to provide reinforcement but delivers those reinforcers at low rates. This program provides an account and a cue to give individual and social reinforcement. One method involves giving the caregiver a *checklist* that requires recording the effects of reinforcement efforts 20 times a day. The responsibility for recording prompts the caregiver to reinforce the client 20 times. An important component of the change program is to involve the caregiver in setting the criteria for change. Another is that the criteria start out low and gradually increase. The more family involvement there is, the higher the likelihood of an effective outcome. The program increases the probability that the reinforcement techniques are properly implemented by the family change agent.

The most structured intervention is the *token economy*. Token economies should only be used when family caregivers experience considerable difficulty in implementing a behavioral technique. The token economy includes points or other ''tokens'' such as chips or coupons, which can later be exchanged for tangible reinforcers. This system provides tangible evidence of delivery of reinforcers. In addition, it provides systematic protocols for the delivery of reinforcers, the methods of delivery, and the value of the reinforcer. Token economies *may* be viable for the impaired elderly residing at home, but research has only begun to evaluate their effectiveness with this population. Nevertheless, when there is family involvement and motivation, token economies may well be effective methods of delivering reinforcers.

PLANNING FOR MAINTENANCE
OF CHANGE

After interventions have been introduced, training has been completed, and it has been ascertained that the caregiver is carrying out the program, two tasks are left. First, the effects of the programs are evaluated, and necessary changes and additions are made. Once it is assured that the program changes have been effective, it is necessary to insure that they will continue to operate in the client's environment. Planning for maintenance of change in effect begins long before planning for case closure. The need for maintenance is a part of the initial assessment. Maintainable procedures must be incorporated into intervention planning and implementation. After maintenance procedures are effectively established, case termination can be planned.

The major task in the maintenance phase is to insure that the appropriate and necessary supports are available for the client to continue achieving an adequate level of reinforcement to live a positive life-style. Maintenance is achieved through systematic fading of components of the intervention rather than abrupt ending of contact, through environmental reprogramming procedures, through insuring that the responsibility for the ongoing interventions is in the hands of the clients, and through insuring that required community services are available and used. Nay (1979) has outlined maintenance procedures as (a) follow-up, (b) retraining, (c) systematic fading of practitioner, and (d) environmental reprogramming.

Each procedure is evaluated to determine the need for maintenance plans and consequent retraining of support persons. Maintenance needs are most clearly evaluated by withdrawing the treatment and observing whether gains are continued. For example, a family who has been using a visiting and telephone schedule to structure their interaction could discontinue weekly scheduling and continue to monitor contacts. If these do not deteriorate, a schedule may no longer be necessary. Very often, however, although the training procedure may no longer be needed, a less intense procedure is necessary to maintain gains.

Fading

A frequent component of maintenance procedures is fading. Fading refers to gradual reduction of the frequency or intensity of a procedure to a level that will still maintain the behavior change. In the example just used, the family might no longer need to make a daily schedule of contacts, but could fade the scheduling to a weekly basis. If successful, the interval between scheduling is faded to alternate weeks or months. The initial fading procedure is taught as part of the treatment completion phase. Families can independently initiate further fading following intervention.

Fading may include decreasing client-practitioner contact, decreasing data collection tasks, or decreasing a component of a specific procedure (as illustrated earlier). Fading of data collection has been feasible with Elderly Support Project clients and helpful as a method of decreasing expected activities of clients or support people as intervention goals are met. Data collection forms may be simplified over time. For example, forms may be reduced from a comprehensive activity checklist to focus on more limited targets. Similarly, data collection in later phases may be reduced from daily to fewer times per week. When behavior change is maintained, collection may be cut to once per week and later eliminated. Data collection may be resumed for follow-up verification. In work to date, however, clients have occasionally persisted in collecting behavioral data after the contract for data collection has expired or been renegotiated.

Fading of intervention may require special consideration. A working principle is that using fading of intervention should not decrease the overall amount of reinforcement available to the clients or support persons. One must therefore be hesitant to ask families to decrease reinforcement, positive attention, or reward-related cues, as the availability was so limited and implementing simple praise often required considerable training. It is not the reinforcement that is the target of fading, but the delivery system for the reinforcement. For example, a contract to thank an elderly father each time he makes a telephone call may be faded or dropped; the appreciation for the call has not decreased. If calls decrease subsequently, however, the procedure (or a part of it) may need to be reinstated.

Fading of practitioner contact is an inherent part of termination or case transition procedures. Whereas the client may see the practitioner daily or several times a week in early phases, by middle phases this might be limited to every week or so. In later phases the frequency of contact can be faded to every 3 or 4 weeks, then systematically to every 6 or 8 weeks. By continuing contact, the practitioner ascertains if the behavior change has been maintained and provides additional support or training as needed. A criterion often used for case termination is 2 months of successful goal achievement, followed by monthly follow-up telephone calls.

Environmental Reprogramming

Environmental reprogramming refers to the modification of the client's environment so that it continues to foster behavior change after intervention. Environmental reprogramming can be achieved in several ways. The major method used in this approach is the training of support persons in behavioral techniques so they can continue to monitor behavior and implement changes. Because the training occurs in the client's home, and responsibility for implementing procedures is taught to client and support persons on an ongoing basis, the need for programming the transfer of learning of treatment effects may be minimized.

Baer and Wolf (1970) described the procedure of setting a behavioral trap, where contingencies are rearranged to insure continued reinforcement of appropriate behavior, assuring behavioral maintenance. Several kinds of environmental arrangements can be programmed. Physical changes include changes in furniture to promote more self-initiated behavior. For example, with a man who had difficulty with falling, practitioners observed that falls occurred often when he got out of his chair. Family agreed to provide a higher chair with pillows on it, enabling him to get out of the chair more safely. Consequently he was able to transfer from the chair independently.

Similarly, efforts to relocate the individual to another setting, either for a few hours or permanently, are a form of environmental reprogramming. Social changes in the environment may include introducing new people into the setting, increasing the frequency of visiting, and introducing access to outside services or agencies through community service linkages.

Note that most of these suggestions are often viewed as intervention procedures. In effect, maintenance occurs throughout intervention and is a criterion in selecting interventions.

Program Transfer

Program transfer refers to transferring responsibility for program design to clients or to support persons. Transferring the program is in effect reprogramming the environment. During the maintenance phase the practitioner takes less active responsibility for treatment development and monitoring, training clients to increase their involvement in this regard.

It is often possible to transfer program responsibility from the practitioner to the support person. One method of doing this is through formal instruction of behavior principles to the client. A portion of contact may include teaching the client the function and techniques of using reinforcement, shaping, and cues. Although research in applying didactic training to family members has been developed with other age groups (O'Dell, O'Quin, Alford, O'Briant, & Giebenhain, 1982), specific evaluation is needed for application to older families.

More often family members assume program responsibility through formal and informal contracting. Whereas the practitioner initially collects data, the caregivers take over implementation. Whereas the practitioner initially contracts with the older person directly for activity, in later phases the practitioner instructs the caregiver to renegotiate contracts. Whereas the practitioner initially calls to remind the client of an agreement to go to an activity center, the family may assume this responsibility when the habit becomes established. Ideally all responsibilities are initially taught to family members, and the practitioner then functions in an advisory capacity. With individualized clients, however, the amount of program responsibility given to the clients is often varied according to their interest, performance, and reinforcement levels.

The older individual may learn to take program responsibility also, even though behavior problems may be evident. In many cases caregivers began as primary data collectors, only to be replaced or supplemented by clients directly recording data later on. Clients' participatory abilities are often underestimated. Similarly the clients are often the best sources of the terms of specific contracts.

COMMUNITY SERVICE LINKAGES

Community service linkages refer to any ongoing participation or contact with a service agency outside the home. Often, however, clients need assistance in learning about service linkages. Community service linkages are defined as strategies for increasing the amount of reinforcement available to an older person on an ongoing basis. Linkages may include increased family contact or medical care, as well as community service agencies. Although they may often be implemented as initial or preliminary interventions, or even as primary interventions, linkages are included as part of maintenance procedures to stress the need to ascertain ongoing reinforcement after the practitioner leaves the scene.

When to Link

A number of criteria are important in determining when to foster community linkages. Services available to the client are assessed in initial interviews. A formal assessment can emphasize identifying service supports, or this information can be conveyed informally. Second, the necessary services are assessed. As goals and desirable outcomes are formulated, the practitioner considers what outside sources of help may foster increased activity or happiness. Third, the practitioner assesses what behaviors are required for service participation. Will an individual need to learn to negotiate a bus system in order to get to a doctor or an educational program? Will a client need to be continent to participate in a day center or sheltered workshop? Will the client need to be able to answer the telephone to use a telephone reassurance program or answer the door to let in a home health aide?

The fourth criterion related to behaviors needed is: What services are necessary to maintain behavior change? If a person has learned to increase his or her social conversation, what service will be required to maintain this increase in conversation? Put differently, how can the practitioner and the family assure that people will be around to talk to the person and thereby reinforce his or her need for conversation (and intellectual stimulation)? Is there a social club or senior activity group that could be joined? Is transportation available? How does the relationship to such services need to be monitored to assure continued involvement?

A major consideration is the impact of service changes on intervention evaluation. If the homemaker who has been assisting Mrs. Jones changes, the practitioner needs to consider this in evaluating the clients' self-care activities. If the physician changes medications, the practitioner may notice more or less independent care or even provide data to document side effects.

In fact, evaluation is an important component of service linkages. A service linkage requires the same careful monitoring as a behavioral intervention to insure successful implementation and effectiveness. Each service should serve a behavioral function—to increase or maintain something needed by the client. Home health services can maintain self-care skills, social interaction, and physical needs. Transportation can maintain out-

of-home activity. Evaluation designs applied to other behaviors can be applied to service evaluation as well (although the services may in effect be
intervention packages that are somewhat complex to assess). The collection of baseline data on a problem for which community service is sought
can precede service initiation. AB designs can be used to evaluate the success of a service on some specific behavior. For example, one client, Mrs.
White, complained constantly, particularly about physical symptoms. Her
husband learned to record her complaining daily. After she began in a
day-care program, her husband's data collection confirmed that her complaining was less of a problem. (See Figure 6.1 for task work sheet.)

Linkage Procedures

In the Elderly Support Project a 7-step linkage procedure has been
adapted from Weissman's work (1976). Specific work sheets to evaluate
service programs and to monitor the linkage process are used. Linkage
steps include problem identification, resource location, option exploration,
resource selection, resource connection, verification or resource assistance,
and follow-up/evaluation.

Sources of Service Linkage Information

Work with the elderly requires the development and constant updating
of files on individual and community resources. Networking is an essential source of current and qualitative information about resources.

Certainly community information programs include information about
services for senior citizens. Area Agency on Aging offices often provide
useful referral information. Often, however, clients need assistance in a
personalized resource search. Clients themselves often are good sources
of information about what is available to them. Clients or family members
may or may not be able to pay for services—a factor that must be taken
into account. Often family and friends are available to provide services.
Churches and community contacts may be of help as well.

More than occasionally, the required service cannot be located for the
client. At these times the practitioner, the client, and the family think together about temporary or longer-term methods and attempt to design
an alternative.

TERMINATION AND FOLLOW-UP

When intervention is successful, service to the client is not actually ter-
minated. Visitation ceases, but training has produced learning and habit
changes that assure that services will continue to be used. The goal of
interventions is to structure ongoing sources of reinforcement for the

clients and to do what is possible to see that clients retain these after contact with the practitioner is discontinued.

As contact is discontinued with clients, a method to assure systematic follow-up is put in place. Telephone follow-up begins on a monthly basis, and then is faded to semimonthly and, finally, quarterly. Follow-up continues for at least one year following termination.

Follow-ups include some reassessment of client and support person functioning, perhaps using posttest instruments or consumer satisfaction interviews. Presence of target behaviors are reassessed, and retraining is provided as needed.

A second kind of follow-up involves the availability of practitioners to answer questions and receive program reports following termination. Because the clients are elderly, and often deprived socially, provision for ongoing social contact is an essential part of this approach.

Chapter 5
Evaluation of Intervention as a Practice Innovation

Evaluation of intervention procedures is critical to family practice with older people. This evaluation not only enables the practitioner to determine the effects of interventions, but it also teaches the clients and caregivers to evaluate the effectiveness of agency staff. Evaluation allows the continued development and refinement of interventions that enables practitioners to continually improve their efforts. As home care to older people is still an emerging set of techniques, this ongoing evaluation remains crucial to the development of geriatric practice.

The best fit between clients and interventions can be developed using single-case evaluation. This methodology is appropriate for evaluating clinical interventions and is the product of the applied behavior analysis literature (Baer et al., 1968; Hersen & Barlow, 1976). It is being used extensively in clinical practice situations (Jayaratne & Levy, 1979; Pinkston et al., 1982). The single-case designs presented in this chapter include the clinical baseline intervention comparison, clinical multiple-baseline intervention, intervention-reversal, changing-criteria, multiple-baseline-across-behaviors, multiple-baseline-across-settings, multiple-baseline-across-clients, and multiple-replication designs. These single-case designs are supplemented by pre-post and group comparisons, although usually the practitioner will not be able to use the random selection of clients required by these designs.

Distinctively, the evaluation in this approach has great utility for both caregivers and clients by showing the importance of the intervention and by allowing them to compare their current efforts with their previous attempts to solve the problems. This comparison provides an additional reason for them to continue to use the procedures and should enhance maintenance of treatment effects.

The data provide the means for continued development and refinement of the procedures and enable more immediate improvement in the treatment effort. This is particularly useful as practitioners adapt clinical and community linkage procedures to the requirements of the elderly population, because the decisions of this emerging technology can be informed by data.

Further evaluation is an ongoing component of interviews, which as a matter of course include regular data review with the clients. To be certain that observed changes in problem behaviors are related to the intervention, evaluations may be varied and the behavioral levels compared across various conditions. This makes it possible to analyze each treatment plan and to evaluate separate components when it is important to identify the effectiveness of specific intervention components.

CLINICAL BASELINE
INTERVENTION COMPARISON

The basis of single-case designs is a comparison of problem measures during baseline (before intervention) with problem measures during and after intervention. These comparisons allow judgements to be made regarding any changes in the problem behavior associated with the onset of the intervention. The comparison of these two conditions frequently aids the practitioner in selecting clinical options and in the evaluation of the outcome, but it can also guide the practitioner in finding a better intervention remedy for a problem. For instance, an increase in the rate of a behavior might indicate increased reinforcers, while a decrease might indicate that reinforcers are not being applied consistently or that consequences are possibly punishing. No change could imply that the consequences or cues included in the intervention are neutral.

Because baseline data consist of repeated measures of the same behavior over several days, the practitioner can evaluate the trend, or pattern, of occurrence of problem behaviors. The measures used are usually the intensity, frequency, and duration of a behavior. That is, how often does it occur, how serious is it, and how long does it last? The pattern includes the direction in which the behavior is going before intervention, whether it is increasing or decreasing along any of the dimensions just listed. As described in chapters 3 and 4, graphs are useful in assessing the findings, and they are usually used as part of the intervention.

The comparison between baseline and intervention data is the minimal design. It can be helpful in evaluating whether or not a change has occurred but not, however, in determining what caused the change. This initial comparison is the first step in all of the following single-case designs.

An example of clinical baseline intervention is found in chapter 6, Practice Illustration 2, the Thomas case (see Figure 6.2), which compares a baseline of self-care with that of intervention. In addition to this simple design, several variations might be useful for clinicians. For instance, the first intervention may not be successful, and a second may be desirable without the necessity of returning to the baseline condition. Therefore the practitioner could compare Intervention 2 to both the ineffective first intervention, as baseline, and the previous baseline (that is, A, B1, B2, etc.). This would continue until an effective intervention was found.

Clinical Multiple-Baseline Intervention

Because it is usual that, in addition to a decrease in undesirable behaviors, the rates of desirable behavior need to be increased, a second clinical design is suggested. This design, the clinical multiple-baseline (see Table 5.1A), monitors two behaviors during baseline, one to be decreased and one to be increased. Intervention is introduced first on one behavior and then on the other at different times, and the effects are noted on both. With elderly clients it is particularly important to include evaluation of a positive behavior as well as a negative behavior, as a way of insuring that positive reinforcement is maintained or increased for people who are socially deprived, which includes most impaired elderly clients. This is described more fully by Pinkston and her colleagues in chapter 4 of their book (Pinkston et al., 1982). This is a particularly useful design for training caregivers because it shapes them to define positive behaviors to monitor as well as negative ones and serves as a reminder to the practitioner too.

Intervention-Reversal Design

With this design, conditions are contrasted to determine changes in client responses. In its most basic form, the design begins with Condition A, the collection of baseline data, to measure a stable operant level of the target behavior. The B condition, intervention, is then implemented, and a comparison to Condition A shows related changes. Experimental control is then tested by a reversal to Condition A to indicate the probability that the intervention procedure was functional in changing client behavior. Removal of the intervention procedures and return to baseline procedures and related behavior changes support or deny treatment effect. Another replication of Condition B strengthens the causal inferences that can be made in addition to leaving the client appropriately in the treatment condition. Often a maintenance condition, B1, follows, which includes fading out the intensive intervention procedures or the development of a program to maintain the improved response (see Table 5.1B).

Table 5.1. Single-Case Designs

A. CLINICAL MULTIPLE-BASELINE

Behavior	I	Phase II	III	IV
Excess Behavior	Baseline	Intervention	Intervention	Follow-up
Deficit Behavior	Baseline	Baseline	Intervention	Follow-up

B. INTERVENTION-REVERSAL

I	II	Phase III	IV	V
Baseline	Treatment	Baseline	Treatment	Maintenance

C. CHANGING-CRITERIA

I	II	III	Phase IV	V	VI
Baseline	Treatment (Criterion 1)	Treatment (Criterion 2)	Treatment (Criterion 3)	Treatment (Criterion 4)	Maintenance

D. MULTIPLE-BASELINE-ACROSS-BEHAVIORS

Behavior	I	Phase II	III	IV	V
Social Interaction	Baseline	Treatment	Treatment	Treatment	Maintenance
Medication	Baseline	Baseline	Treatment	Treatment	Maintenance
Eating	Baseline	Baseline	Baseline	Treatment	Maintenance

E. MULTIPLE-BASELINE-ACROSS-SETTINGS

Setting	I	Phase II	III	IV	V
Own Home	Baseline	Treatment	Treatment	Treatment	Maintenance
Son's Home	Baseline	Baseline	Treatment	Treatment	Maintenance
Group	Baseline	Baseline	Baseline	Treatment	Maintenance

F. MULTIPLE-BASELINE-ACROSS-CLIENTS

Client	I	Phase II	III	IV	V
Daughter	Baseline	Treatment	Treatment	Treatment	Maintenance
Son-in-law	Baseline	Baseline	Treatment	Treatment	Maintenance
Sister	Baseline	Baseline	Baseline	Treatment	Maintenance

G. MULTIPLE-REPLICATION

	I	Phase II	III	IV	V
Client 1	Baseline	Intervention			
Client 2		Baseline	Intervention		
Client 3				Baseline	Intervention

This design is used with variations: for example, a series of treatments may be implemented in steps to achieve a specific effect, each of which would be represented by subsequent replication of Bs, that is, $ABB^1B^2B^3$. In cases where immediate intervention is necessary because of emergency situations, BAB designs may be implemented. Intrasubject replication is used when it provides important educational information to the family and when discontinuing treatment is an inevitable treatment phase or clearly will not harm the client.

CHANGING-CRITERIA DESIGNS

These designs provide some experimental control for stepwise intervention. After collection of baseline data, an intervention program is implemented in steps, with specific target criteria for each step. After each designated criterion, a stepwise change in criterion rate is applied during succeeding intervention phases (Hall, 1971; Reid & Smith, 1981). Each phase of behavior serves as a baseline for the subsequent intervention phase. Experimental control is enhanced through successive replication of reaching target behaviors (Kratochwill, 1978). Kratochwill suggests that four replications are necessary to establish experimental control. The design is presented in Table 5.1C.

Alternative designs, characterized by simultaneous data collection on a number of components, are categorized as multiple-baseline designs. These designs allow replication of the techniques without reversal of treatment procedures (Baer, 1973). Multiple-baseline designs involve maintaining a constant treatment procedure while varying behavior, subjects, or setting (Baer et al., 1968; Hersen & Barlow, 1976; Jayaratne & Levy, 1979; Risley & Wolf, 1972).

MULTIPLE-BASELINE-ACROSS-
BEHAVIORS DESIGNS

These designs are useful when target behaviors occur independently from each other. With this design, the same treatment is applied in sequence to several behaviors, while the baseline conditions are held constant on the untreated behaviors. For example, if a client has identified target behaviors that include low rates of social interaction, medication management problems, and inappropriate use of eating utensils, a possible treatment technique to test is the use of oral prompts or stimulus cues. This involves instructing the caregiver to begin prompting social interaction while continuing to react to medication and eating problems as previously. When the desired effect is noted, the support persons are instructed to implement the prompt procedures for both the interaction and the medication behaviors. When those behaviors have changed, the procedure is then applied to use of eating utensils. This design is outlined in Table 5.1D.

As shown in Phase V of Table 5.1D, following the treatment of all three targeted behaviors, a maintenance procedure is introduced to extend the effectiveness of the treatment, thereby providing an ongoing prosthetic environment for the client. This maintenance procedure is similar to one developed by Blackman et al. (1979) in their program to maintain use of utensils.

MULTIPLE-BASELINE-ACROSS-SETTINGS DESIGN

This design offers opportunities to test the effectiveness and generality of treatment procedures in several settings and to program generality when it does not occur. With this design, after recording of baseline data in several settings, intervention is implemented serially across different settings. The effect of the treatment on the same behavior can then be examined in different environments. For example, if a client has a low rate of talking with family in his or her own home, the home of a child, and when attending a senior citizens group, an intervention technique (for example, prompt and praise) can be tested serially in each setting.

As shown in Table 5.1E, Phase V, following the treatment of all three targeted settings, a maintenance procedure is introduced to extend treatment gains.

MULTIPLE-BASELINE-ACROSS-CLIENTS DESIGN

This design is most appropriate when interaction among clients in the same setting is minimal or does not occur. It is suitable when a client is being taught to change social interactions with different family members.

The design provides procedures for ongoing evaluation of intervention with multiple behaviors, clients, or settings; however, it lacks the excellent experimental control of the multiple family members (in such cases the family members become the clients within the design). For example, a daughter, son-in-law, and sister might be taught, serially, to reinforce appropriate verbalizations of an older person. The subsequent success of the treatment with each additional family member would then provide additional experimental control and reduce alternative explanations for improved social verbalizations. This design, which provides an interclient replication, is depicted in Table 5.1F.

MULTIPLE-REPLICATION DESIGN

This design allows the practitioner to replicate a procedure across several behaviors, clients, or settings. It is a clinically useful design because it allows some replication of intervention effects without the constraints of multiple baselines being recorded at the same time by the caregiver or the necessity of starting all of the client baselines at the same time, an unusual practice opportunity with seriously impaired clients (Table 5.1G). Certainly, this design lacks the experimental control of the multiple-baseline designs, but it facilitates careful monitoring of client progress in a systematic way through several interventions (see Pinkston et al., 1982, for a more complete description of this design). In the Keller case in chapter 6 (Figure 6.5) the practitioner was able to monitor four contractual interventions with the caregiver, three involving the client's behaviors and one involving family members' behavior. Change in this case was not dramatic, but overall progress was evident on the larger multiple-intervention graph.

The foregoing designs are used individually and in combination to evaluate behavioral treatment techniques for older people and their supporting persons. Using these designs may seem troublesome to practitioners unaccustomed to using systematic data analysis, but the payoffs for clients, caregivers, and practitioners are high. Looking at evidence of improvement on paper is a motivating experience for clients and caregivers. Absence of improvement is even more important to note at once and is motivating to the practitioner.

SUMMARY

The practitioner, as he or she begins to review a number of cases, may begin to generalize about the effectiveness of procedures for a variety of clients. As the practitioner tests and retests a specific set of procedures over a number of cases, he or she engages in multiple replications of effects. These replications are called *systematic replication* (Hersen & Barlow, 1976; Sidman, 1960). The practice illustrations in the next chapter exemplify systematic replications with the impaired elderly and support the general nature of these procedures for that group.

Chapter 6

Application of Behavioral Procedures to Specific Problems

Because family concerns about older relatives encompass many needs and problems, including specific behavior problems, we have outlined a method that families can use to ameliorate behavior problems in order to maximize use of existing resources, improve interaction, and, it is hoped, increase family satisfaction. More complete examples are delineated for the practitioner to use to teach families to increase rates of social contacts, self-care routines, meaningful activities, and positive verbal behaviors.

INCREASING SOCIAL CONTACTS

Isolation and withdrawal from community and family living are problems that beset older citizens. Social isolation may occur because of too few opportunities for socialization. Low rates of social skills may be related to physical or social losses, too few sufficient reinforcers following social participation to sustain further socialization, or both. Older persons and their families may require assistance to determine reasonable levels of social engagement. For some, who previously had many social contacts, physical changes related to aging may mean that simple involvement in daily activities is so taxing that social efforts need to be reduced. For others, who have retired and are still able to meet their daily social and physical needs, old age may be at a time of emptiness, and social activities may need to be increased. Although the need for social contact is crucial for all ages, the amount and kind can change over time. Often it is assumed that contacts with friends and family are satisfying, when in reality the visits are unpleasant to family members. One such case presents an extreme example: An elderly woman was deprived of social interaction, even though she lived with her daughter and granddaughter.

Procedures for improving social contacts are outlined in Table 6.1. The desired social-contact activity is first defined by discussing what activities the family prefers. A reinforcement inventory might be used to suggest the range of activities enjoyed by various family members. Available and

Table 6.1. Intervention Procedures: Increasing Social Contacts

STEP	IMPLEMENTATION
1. Defining desired behavior	1. Select a specific behavioral outcome, using baseline data and assessment data to determine low-frequency activities involving others. Check the behavior with family and client to verify its social and clinical relevance. Define the desired outcome in operational terms.
2. Evaluating resources required to achieve desired social contacts	2. Resources required may include transportation from relatives or agencies, funds, and cues to elicit necessary behaviors.
3. Selecting desired time, place, and components of the social contact	3. Discuss possible times and places when the social contacts may occur and steps the client will need to engage in (i.e., getting dressed, arranging for transport, going to activity).
4. Eliciting agreement to engage in activity	4. Present one or more possible target activities to the client, along with discussion and explanation of the time, place, and resources available and the behavioral components. Ask the client if he or she is willing to participate. Enlist involved relatives in providing resources, participating, and reinforcing client's agreement to participate.
5. Specifying the contract in writing	5. Once agreed upon, formalize the contract in verbal and written form. Use either a task assignment contract or an individualized contract to state the specific activity agreed upon, who will do what to achieve it, and when this will occur. Give a copy to each participant.
6. Rehearsing components of the social contacts	6. Have the family practice the required steps to achieve the social contacts.
7. Prompting social contacts	7. Incorporate a variety of possible reminders or prompts including (a) calendar notes/appointment books, (b) reminder telephone calls from practitioner or family members, (c) verbal prompts from those living with clients.

(continued)

Table 6.1. (*continued*)

STEP	IMPLEMENTATION
8. Reinforcing social contacts immediately	8. Teach available caregivers to notice, call attention to, and praise social contacts when these occur and to avoid complaining about the client's not engaging in desired contacts.
9. Recording	9. Have caregivers note social contacts on recording forms.
10. Monitoring and providing feedback	10. Review the data at least once a week and provide verbal praise for task adherence.
11. Renegotiating the contract	11. If task adherence does not occur, review each step of the procedure and suggest and recontract for necessary changes.
12. Recontracting	12. When adherence does occur, consider the need to recontract to achieve additional outcomes.

needed resources are then evaluated, and additional resources are secured, if necessary. A contract is then developed that includes agreement from relevant family members to engage in specific activities. It is useful to specify the contract in writing and rehearse necessary components of the social contacts. Reminders or prompts are used to insure that all concerned remember to do the tasks needed to achieve the contract. The family is taught to attend or to reward appropriate social contacts. Finally, the contract is implemented, evaluated, and renegotiated if needed.

Practice Illustration 1: Using Contracts to Increase Independence and Social Contacts Practitioner/Researchers: Glenn R. Green and Christine Marlow

Mrs. Banks was a 67-year-old divorcee who had worked as a farm and domestic worker in addition to raising several children. About a year previously, she had moved to a new city to be nearer her children, in response to their concerns about her abilities for self-care. She first lived in an apartment near her son, but later moved in with her daughter and granddaughter to provide baby-sitting help and to receive help from them.

At referral, Mrs. Banks was hospitalized because of her "paranoid behaviors,'' which occurred in her daughter's home. These behaviors included accusations, frequent swearing and shouting, refusal to take medication, and reported hallucinations. Mrs. Banks had a diagnosis of ''stable dementia'' and apparent memory problems. She was reported to be illiterate.

Two primary caregivers and one secondary caregiver were involved with Mrs. Banks. Her daughter reported providing food, shelter, transportation, financial help, and supervision for her mother. The daughter worked during the day and had little direct contact with her mother. Mrs. Banks' granddaughter spent some time with her each day, and no specific problems were noted with this contact. Mrs. Banks also had a son who lived two miles from the family but had contact with her less than once a month.

During assessment interviews, Mrs. Banks indicated that she would like to go to a club or organization weekly, to the store two or three times a week, and out for daily walks. The long-range intervention goal was to increase Mrs. Banks' contact with the community. Three immediate steps to help her achieve that goal were (a) linkage to a day-service program, (b) attempts to increase contact with her son, and (c) a move to her own apartment.

The family recorded the frequency of her appropriate talking, swearing, and talking to herself on a Family Behavior Record. Mrs. Banks exhibited a low rate of appropriate talk, swearing, and instances of talking to herself during an initial baseline phase.

A day center was located and application made, but linkage was not completed. Initially, admission was not possible because of funding problems, and later, when service was offered, she refused to participate. The family then decided that a move by Mrs. Banks to her own apartment was desired. It was clear that with the daughter and granddaughter out of the home so much, Mrs. Banks did not have opportunities for social interaction and that she did not feel she could engage in household tasks while she lived with them. It was felt by Mrs. Banks and by her son and daughter that appropriate financial resources were available for the move and that the adult children could provide enough help to sustain independent living. Although hallucinations and bizarre behaviors were the initial referring problems, early data showed that they were not major problems, but rather that Mrs. Banks' extreme social deprivation was more serious.

Family contracts were developed and recorded on a task assignment sheet (Figure 6.1). This work sheet was used to establish contractual agreements between family members and the practitioner, to record data on completion of assigned tasks, and to provide feedback to the family for successful task completion. In addition, the family recorded frequency of social contacts by noting the frequency of visitors and visits out of the home.

FIGURE 6.1. Task assignment work sheet (selected entries)

Client: Mrs. Banks
Major objective of tasks: Moving into own apartment
Steps: Criteria to be achieved before moving to next step
Tasks: Specific activities to be achieved by each individual, specified in behavioral terms

Step: Find suitable apartment. Date begun: 1/22 Done:1/29					
Task	Client Mrs. B.	Relative 1 Daughter	Relative 2 Grand- daughter	Relative 3 Son	Practitioner
1	Go with grand-daughter on Sunday to get three papers	Ask friend about realtor to contact	Go with grandmother on Sunday	Look for apartment nearby	Check college newspaper and bring to next meeting
Done	1/29	1/27	1/29		1/24
2	Call one apartment and find out details	Call and find out when listings come out			Look in neigh-borhood for signs, and call if any are located
Done		1/27			1/27
3	Go with daughter to look at apart-ments	Get list on Saturday and note suitable ones			
Done	1/29	1/28			
4		Go with mother to see apartments			
Done		1/29			

Initial tasks that were delineated included the specific steps of finding information about particular apartments, visiting the apartments, and making arrangements for moving. Intervention steps included (a) review of achievements on previous tasks, (b) praise from the practitioner for task completion, (c) analysis of incomplete tasks and remaining activities, and (d) formulation of steps and tasks for the next week.

By the third week, all tasks were completed, and an apartment was rented. The move occurred one month later. Task assignment work sheet results indicated that 95% of tasks were completed by participants. During this time conversational patterns improved notably. Talking to herself, the client's major referral behavior, ceased almost entirely. Appropriate conversation increased moderately during the planning phase.

Subsequent to the move, new data-recording procedures were initiated. Mrs. Banks noted each time a visitor came to the apartment and each time she talked on the telephone. Although she was functionally illiterate, she was able to keep tallies of these behaviors as well as to monitor her medication. The practitioner then met with both son and daughter and established a social contact schedule with them. Both agreed to call regularly, and the daughter agreed to take her mother shopping once weekly and to church twice monthly. The son agreed to visit twice a month. The contract was put into written form, and results were monitored in the next few weeks. Figure 6.2 shows results of the intervention. Although trips out of the home did not improve notably during the contracting period,

FIGURE 6.2. Mrs. Banks' weekly frequency of visitors and telephone calls

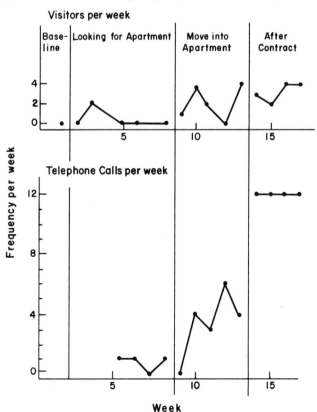

visits per week did increase from none to an average of 2.6 visits per week during the search for an apartment. After the move, visits increased to over 3 per week, an average of one every other day. Telephone calls increased more dramatically, from 0–1 calls per day to almost 2 per day, during the postcontract period.

Follow-up reports indicated that Mrs. Banks talked to her granddaughter and daughter daily. She visited with her daughter 2 or 3 times per week and with her son on a weekly basis. To date, Mrs. Banks has maintained her apartment and her family contact patterns for over 3 years.

In this case Mrs. Banks' family upgraded their evaluation of her abilities through discussions with the practitioner such that independent living became a possible option for her. The use of structured contracts helped the family plan and carry out Mrs. Banks' move. Monitoring and programming of social contacts after the move was probably the most important intervention component. Without such monitoring, Mrs. Banks' level of reinforcement and activity might have become so low that new behavior problems could have emerged in an effort to attract some social attention. The contracting procedure led to contacts at least twice a day, as well as to support for out-of-home activity. Clearly, these interventions might have determined whether or not Mrs. Banks could continue to live alone. In effect, independent living promoted more social opportunities for Mrs. Banks than did living with her family. It immediately gave Mrs. Banks a meaningful activity to plan for and engage in, while providing opportunity for independent activities and privacy.

IMPROVING SELF-CARE

Self-care deficits among the elderly include losses in ability to dress, to eat independently, to maintain hygiene behaviors, and to use toilet facilities appropriately. Self-care deficits can be related to physical changes such as ambulation problems, tremors, and coordination difficulties. Often, however, self-care deficiencies arise when memory or cognitive organization declines. Then the cause is an inability to remember the time and procedural steps required to complete the task, rather than physical disability. A person may be able to go to the washroom adequately, but may not respond to bodily or temporal cues and therefore becomes incontinent. In long-term facilities an individual may be denied opportunity for adequate self-care through restraints or lack of resources. Families may learn to provide appropriate cues, reinforce, and attend appropriately to self-care efforts. Two case illustrations are presented. The first is Mrs. Thomas, who had a low level of personal care, particularly dressing and hygiene. The second case is Mr. Raven, who was incontinent.

A general self-care procedure is illustrated in Table 6.2. For each activity a specific desired behavior is defined and broken down into necessary sub-

Table 6.2. Intervention Procedures: Self-care Behavior

STEP	IMPLEMENTATION
1. Defining desired behavior	1. Select specific behavioral outcome (i.e., client will dress in underwear, slacks, shirt, shoes, and socks, etc.; client will wash face 3 times a day; client will use washroom 4 times a day).
2. Setting and using a schedule	2. Designate a time to begin and end each occurrence of self-care.
3. Providing response opportunity	3. Arrange or ask client to arrange materials (e.g., clothing, soap, and towel) so that they are usable and within easy reach.
4. Prompting correct behavior	4. Have the support person prompt the client to go through each step of the task in the correct order. If there is no response the prompt is repeated once or twice, then two minutes later if necessary.
5. Allowing time for behavior to occur	5. If the client is attempting to complete a self-care task, instruct the caregiver to wait until the task is completed. This should occur within five minutes.
6. Praise appropriate behavior	6. If the client is able to complete the task, the caregiver offers praise or touching (food, token, or point on the recording form may also be used) and then prompts the client to go on to the next step.
7. Assistance if the behavior does not occur	7. If the client does not respond to the prompt within 30 seconds, the caregiver guides the older person through the various steps required. The caregiver provides help with any items the client is unable to complete because of physical impairment or pain.
8. Ignoring inappropriate behavior	8. If the client engages in inappropriate behavior such as complaining, arguing, or any behaviors that serve to bring about an unnecessary delay in the process, the caregiver should remove their attention from the client until the behavior ceases. Caregiver then returns to Step 4.
9. Recording	9. Behavior is recorded on recording form.

steps. A time schedule specifies both the frequency and the duration of the desired activities. Actual interventions are providing an opportunity for the activity to occur, prompting correct attempts to engage in the activity, praising gradual achievement of each step, and using primary rewards, touch, and assisting when necessary. Inappropriate behaviors are ignored, and results of each trial are recorded, so that success can be evaluated and procedures changed if need be.

Practice Illustration 2:
Promoting Self-Care
With an Older Couple
Practitioner/Researcher: Glenn R. Green

Mrs. Thomas was a 70-year-old woman who lived in an apartment with her husband. Additional caregivers were three daughters, who visited her several times a week. Mrs. Thomas was affected by dementia, which was manifested by her poor memory and her failure to care for her personal needs. The family was referred because both Mr. and Mrs. Thomas had low levels of activities and problems with self-care. Mr. Thomas' primary self-care difficulty was remembering to complete a spot check of his insulin level four times a day, take injections, and eat a nighttime snack (all necessary for his diabetes).

After an assessment phase, during which the problems were delineated, specific definitions were developed for each problem. Controlling insulin level was defined as checking for sugar in his urine before each meal and snack, injecting insulin once each morning, and eating a bedtime snack. For Mrs. Thomas, personal care was defined as taking a bath, brushing her teeth, brushing her hair, and being dressed for 8 hours a day.

In this case, a simple schedule was set for Mrs. Thomas' behaviors—she was to complete each behavior at least once a day. Hair brushing, bathing, and teeth brushing could occur at any time; dressing must occur early enough for her to be dressed for 8 hours. Mr. Thomas' schedule was more complicated, however. He was to take insulin and check sugar before breakfast; check sugar again before lunch, dinner, and bedtime; and eat a snack at bedtime. Recording was done by Mr. Thomas on daily checklists (see Figure 6.3).

Initial assessment and observations revealed that both Mr. and Mrs. Thomas had the necessary skills to engage in the desired behaviors. For Mrs. Thomas, the needed clothing and equipment were conveniently available. Prompts by family members seemed to be punishing and ineffective. It was decided to try to increase the prompt procedures in an effort to promote Mrs. Thomas' abilities and increase the pleasantness of the situation for all. Mr. Thomas and his daughters agreed to use differential attention to reinforce her positive self-care behaviors. The family praised Mrs. Thomas when she brushed her teeth, when her hair was combed, and when she had taken a bath or was dressed for several hours. They were instructed not to nag her when she did not comply with their wishes and not to give additional instructions or prompts. In this case the intervention emphasized Steps 5, 6, and 8 of the self-care procedures on Table 6.3.

The practitioners assessed the need for increased prompts to help Mr.

FIGURE 6.3. Self-care forms

Mr. Thomas

Sugar check before meal				Breakfast injection		Night snack	
Breakfast	Lunch	Dinner	Snack	Yes	No	Yes	No
Monday							
Tuesday							
Wednesday							
Thursday							
Friday							
Saturday							
Sunday							

Mrs. Thomas

Day	Brush teeth	Brush hair	Bathe	Dressed for over 8 hours
Monday				
Tuesday				
Wednesday				
Thursday				
Friday				
Saturday				
Sunday				

Place an x in the box when the behavior occurs.
If behavior does not occur, leave blank.

Thomas complete his health regimen. Simple signs around the house were used to remind Mr. Thomas to check his urine for sugars at specified times, to take his insulin, and to eat his bedtime snack. These were appropriately placed in the kitchen and the bathroom. Initially a criterion was set for Mr. Thomas to check his sugar level at noon daily.

Findings from the two interventions are illustrated in Figure 6.4. Mrs. Thomas' self-care improved notably, reflecting completion of an average of 2.6 of the required self-care activities during baseline and 3.8 tasks of the 4 (95%) during the intervention phases. She did, however, complete some self-care during all phases and was apparently not as deficient as the family originally reported.

Mr. Thomas' urine checks improved very dramatically. During the baseline phase Mr. Thomas only checked the urine one time (mean = 0.2). During the intervention phase he successfully completed the check on all but 1 of 21 days.

In this case the interventions were evaluated as quite successful. The family, however, continued to seek help in reversing Mrs. Thomas' mem-

FIGURE 6.4. Mrs. Thomas' personal care score and Mr. Thomas' sugar checks

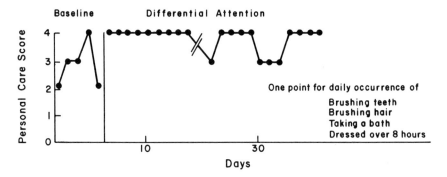

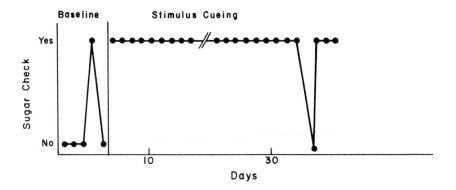

ory problems. Mr. and Mrs. Thomas continued to live at home for 3 years with some help from their daughters and occasional paid staff.

Practice Illustration 3:
Improving Independent Elimination
Practitioner/Researcher:
Rosemary Nelson Young

Mr. Raven, a 66-year-old retiree, was referred by the social worker in a geriatric-psychiatry inpatient program. His history of manic-depressive illness extended back 45 years. His most recent hospitalization had begun 2 months previously, to evaluate possible toxic reactions to his medication (lithium). At referral, weakness in his legs and walking deficits, confusion, familial conflict, and urinary incontinence were identified as possible targets of intervention. He was also diagnosed as having Parkinson's disease.

Mr. Raven and his wife had been married for 47 years, and they lived in a five-room apartment in a residential urban area. Their daughter lived with her family in a city some distance from them and visited only occasionally. She was initially unwilling to increase her support for her parents through participation in the program.

The initial assessments revealed that Mr. Raven was well oriented and fairly satisfied with his social relations, but he stated that he often felt worried and found his life rather routine. He reported few regular activities, hobbies, and personal interests, and he identified three problems of special concern: sleep disturbances, urinary incontinence, and problems with walking. Procedures were developed to improve these and to increase the frequency of his general activities. These procedures illustrate the way in which appropriate elimination can be increased, with a by-product of decreased urinary incontinence.

The medical assessment of his functions revealed no physical cause of his incontinence. Mr. Raven reported that it occurred without warning, failing to provide sufficient physical cues to allow time to walk to the bathroom. Although he had tried to urinate before bed and around mealtimes, no true schedule had been tried.

The Activity Record (Figure 6.5) was adapted to his requirements and used by Mrs. Raven to record baseline information. She recorded frequency of incontinence, appropriate elimination, and several household and social activities hourly. (He was unable or unwilling to record.) Incontinence occurred on an average of one time daily, and Mr. Raven urinated an average of eight times daily.

The general intervention procedures to improve elimination appear in Table 6.3. The procedures were adapted for use with Mr. Raven with the goals of improving elimination and decreasing urinary incontinence. Mrs.

FIGURE 6.5. Filled-in activity record

Date: Wednesday, March 30   Name: Mr. Raven
Recorder: Mrs. Raven

Please check when behaviors occur each hour. Fill out a new sheet each day.

TIME	Walking	In Bed	Out of House	Urination	Household Tasks	TV	Other
7–8 a.m.							
8–9 a.m.							
9–10 a.m.				x			Read
10–11 a.m.		30 min		x			
11–12 a.m.							
12–1 p.m.	x						
1–2 p.m.							
2–3 p.m.	x			IN			
3–4 p.m.						1 hr.	
4–5 p.m.				x			cards
5–6 p.m.							
6–7 p.m.				x			
7–8 p.m.						1 hr.	
8–9 p.m.				x			
9–10 p.m.							
10–11 p.m.				x			
11–12 p.m.							
12–7 a.m.							

x = appropriate
IN = incontinent

Table 6.3. Intervention Procedures:
Elimination Program for Incontinence and Bowel Accidents

STEP	IMPLEMENTATION
1. Defining desired behavior	1. Select a specific behavioral outcome.
2. Setting and using a schedule	2. Using baseline data to select frequency, determine a schedule of intervention. Begin with a frequency that insures *successful* washroom use, usually ½ hour more frequently than reported incontinence or accidents. Often a 1-hour or 1½-hour schedule is used initially. If baseline is inconclusive, begin with a 1½ hour interval and adjust to meet client's needs. Often the schedule can be modified after a few days, based on client performance.
3. Providing response opportunity	3. Provide access to toilet, urinal, or bedpan. May consist of asking if client wants to use washroom, wheeling or walking person to washroom, or giving client urinal or bedpan.
4. Prompting correct behavior	4. Have support person ask client if he or she wishes to use washroom. If response is negative, the prompt is repeated 10 minutes later.
5. Allowing time for behavior to occur	5. If client is ambulatory or mobile without help and able to self-toilet, instruct caregiver to wait at least 5 minutes for response to occur.
6. Praising appropriate behavior	6. If client goes to washroom appropriately, tell caregiver to praise him or her, either verbally or with a material reinforcer (food, token, a point on the recording form). Self-initiated appropriate toilet use is *always* reinforced.
7. Assisting if behavior does not occur	7. If behavior does not occur within 30 minutes or client is incontinent, have caregiver ask client if help is required and provide it (dressing, location, cleaning, etc.). If behavior still does not occur, caregiver waits until next interval and returns to Step 3.
8. Ignoring inappropriate behavior	8. If incontinence or soiling occurs, client instructs caregiver to assist in cleaning up or dressing (or give instructions if client can do so independently). Minimal conversation or physical touch occurs. The change agent should *never* engage in criticism, solicitous conversation, praise, or intense physical contact. Both should ignore the behavior as much as possible.
9. Recording	9. Have the caregiver record behavior on recording form.

Raven agreed to remind her husband to use the washroom every 1½ hours during the day, a schedule that was derived from his baseline rate of urination (12 hours/8 occurrences of urination). This provided a response opportunity for Mr. Raven to urinate appropriately and avoid the discomfort of incontinence. Mrs. Raven was cautioned not to repeat prompts if Mr. Raven did not comply. She agreed to record his behavior without criticism or other consequences. In this sense, then, she was taught to ignore inappropriate behaviors.

A functional analysis of reinforcers showed that for the Ravens, there was neither a need for Mrs. Raven to praise him for appropriate elimination nor any reason to believe that it would be an effective consequence. The Ravens maintained a sense of personal privacy about bathroom behavior, and it was sufficient to remind him to adhere to the schedule. During the weekly sessions with the practitioner, the data were reviewed, and the practitioner praised adherence to the schedule and recording of the data.

With more-impaired individuals, more direct reinforcing consequences may be added, for instance, praise, attention, or material rewards (such as cookies or cigarettes), to effectively encourage improved elimination habits.

Because it was unclear whether or not the Ravens understood the importance of the intervention, a reversal of the procedure was instituted under supervision to encourage them to continue using these procedures following termination. This allowed them to compare the systematic use of the procedure with their former, less systematic methods and to decide how important the scheduling procedures were.

The findings from this evaluated case are presented in Figure 6.6. In this figure the appropriate urinations are presented as percentage of total urinations. Appropriate urination improved from 85% during baseline to 98% during cueing and feedback, decreasing slightly during reversal, moving to 100% during reapplication of cueing and feedback, and continuing at that level during the maintenance phase.

Following this intervention, Mr. Raven began to increase his outside activities briefly, until his wife became ill and he moved in with his daughter, who helped him maintain his appropriate elimination program. He was later rehospitalized and discharged to a nursing home. Efforts to influence staff in these institutions to use the procedures were not successful. Mrs. Raven, however, regained her health and brought Mr. Raven home. Following brief retraining, the procedures were reinstituted and maintained. The Ravens have continued to live independently for a year and have continued to maintain Mr. Raven's appropriate elimination behavior.

This case provides an example of reducing problems associated with toilet use. The caregiver was effectively trained to use systematic pro-

FIGURE 6.6 Mr. Raven's urination behavior

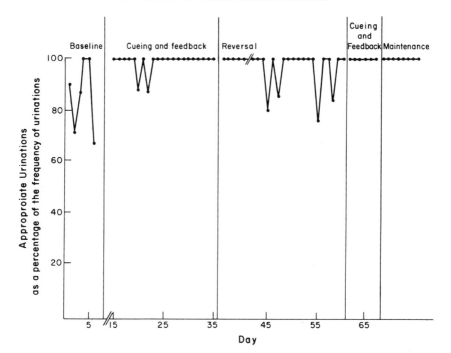

cedures, and the client was then able to engage in other satisfying activities. The caregiver successfully implemented cues, schedules, and reinforcing activities. The client, through his cooperation, was able to avoid noxious consequences.

IMPROVING VERBAL BEHAVIOR

Family caregivers experience communication difficulties as exceedingly frustrating to manage. These verbal problems increase the difficulty of providing care. Conversations between older people and others are sometimes quite limited; families frequently complain that they do not know what to talk about with older, impaired relatives, and they report that they avoid potential encounters. Communication problems often include excessive talking by the older person, including chronic complaints or repetitive statements. Some caregiving spouses complain that they have heard the same story every day of their married lives. Even more upsetting may be the client who perseveres with negative statements that are threatening, embarrassing, or sad such as, "I want to die," "my wife has

another man," or "nobody does anything for me." What are commonly
referred to as hallucinations or memory deficits are viewed as verbal excesses. When persons with Alzheimer's disease or other mental disorders
complain, question, accuse, or hallucinate, families could conclude that
they can do nothing except try to reassure the clients or convince them
that their claims are not so. Research and practice suggest the reinforcing
quality of this response can actually increase both the frequency and intensity of the disorder. Similarly, individuals who are depressed, deficient
in activities or stimulation, and sensorially and socially deprived do not
improve as a result of caregiver rationalizations regarding their pain or
fear, particularly when those rationalizations are their main source of
attention.

An alternative approach (see chapters 2 and 3) for analyzing verbal
deficits includes determination of antecedents, consequences, and alternatives to be reinforced. Socially deprived older people often respond to
questions such as "How are you?" or "What did you do today?" with
a detailed description of their medical conditions and physical or social
complaints. The questions stimulate negative or repetitive responses.
Somewhat different questions or cues may elicit more positive responses,
such as "What would you like to do today?" "You are looking good today" or "Shall we go for a walk?"

Many older adults with behavior problems are bereft of opportunities
to give their opinions, choices, or reports on experiences, and allowing
more opportunity for them to do so may elicit more interesting responses.
Also, clients may not receive adequate consequences for their appropriate
attempts to socialize. A daughter who ignores all attempts of her mother
to engage socially may notice that her mother begins to complain, fanta-
size, verbalize, or escalate positive conversation to an excessive level in
a demand for social attention. Or a spouse that punishes conversation by
saying, "Don't talk to me now. Can't you see that I am busy?" should
expect the usual response to punishment, that is, anger, frustration, fight,
or flight. Finally, the presence of problem verbalizations may imply insufficient activities. Programming alternative activities and reinforcing appropriate behavior while ignoring negative behavior have been supported
by the findings of the Elderly Support Project. The procedures have been
associated with decreases in hallucinations, pain, and complaining.

General procedures for decreasing negative verbalizations are presented
in Table 6.4. Family caregivers are taught to monitor verbal behaviors,
usually for one hour twice a day for high-frequency behaviors and, for
low-rate behaviors, continuously and frequently. A desirable alternative
behavior is defined, and a criterion for reduction of excessive behavior is
selected. In almost all cases alternative behavior is selected to be increased
and maintained. Attention is never withdrawn from negative behaviors

Table 6.4. Intervention Procedures: Decreasing Negative Verbalizations

STEP	IMPLEMENTATION
1. Defining desired behavior	1. Select a specific behavioral outcome, using baseline assessment data to define realistic improvements. Include expected frequency of negative verbalizations and frequency of alternative positive verbalizations (i.e., complaints to be decreased to less than 1 per hour; positive statements increased to 2 per hour).
2. Specifing intervention to be used (differential attention or reinforcement)	2. Adapt the specific procedure and write it down for use in training caregivers. Delineate exactly which behaviors are to be ignored and which are to be attended to or reinforced. Define and illustrate these behaviors. Specify when the procedure is used, by whom, and under what conditions.
3. Training caregivers in use of procedures	3. Introduce caregivers to procedures first through oral and written instructions. Demonstrate how the procedure is used through modeling, illustrating both praise and ignoring. Give family members an opportunity to rehearse the procedure, first acting as the client while the practitioner models and then acting as themselves while practitioner acts as client. Caregivers then practice the procedure with the client while practitioner monitors, giving cues or feedback as needed.
4. Explaining procedure to client and eliciting consent	4. Inform the client of the procedure and give him or her opportunities to ask questions and to agree to participate. If the client objects to the procedure, introduce necessary changes.
5. Setting criteria for ignoring and praising, if needed	5. Specify criteria for use of the intervention; negotiate if necessary.
6. Recording	6. Have the client note praise, ignoring, reinforcers, and positive and negative responses on the recording form.
7. Monitoring and feedback	7. At least once a week review data and provide verbal praise for using the procedures. Offer additional training as needed.

before attention is provided to a positive counterpart. This avoids forcing clients to develop other behaviors, possibly negative, to gain attention, and, instead, allows practitioners and caregivers to shape attractive pro-social behaviors that are likely to increase clients' total social contacts. It may be necessary to build up positive behaviors before ignoring negative, to avoid leaving clients in a state of deprivation.

The procedures in the table specify training methods for teaching caregivers to use differential attention (reinforcement). It is necessary to define the behavior, practice it with the caregiver, observe the caregiver using the procedures with the client, and provide corrective feedback on the performance of the procedures. Both client and caregiver are praised for their attempts to cooperate with the program and for precise implementation of procedures. The practitioner always articulates what was particularly well done by the caregiver and the client. Monitoring, continuing data recording, and single-subject evaluation designs are used to determine changes that need to be made, improvements, and outcome.

Practice Illustration 4:
Reduction of Problem Verbalizations
Practitioner/Researcher: John Schipke

Mr. Brooks, a 73-year-old man living with his wife, had a history of alcohol abuse, anemia, memory and behavior problems, and confusion. The medical diagnosis was Senile Dementia, Alzheimer's type. The major problems identified by the hospital social worker for modification were paranoid statements, verbal abuse of his wife, and inability to remember. He was also diagnosed as having lymphoma, but he refused chemotherapy.

The assessment confirmed his mental impairment and verbal problems, and two types of verbal statements were defined and recorded. Mrs. Brooks completed a daily log recording occurrence and duration of both worried statements and positive or neutral statements (see Figure 6.7 for recording form). Worried statements were defined as statements that showed approval, recognition, praise, or neutral contact. Recording was completed during three 1-hour periods each day. Mrs. Brooks also recorded antecedent conditions for the verbalizations and her response (praise, ignoring, punishing, requesting him to do something else, or other response). The accuracy and reliability of the recording was tested via audiotapes and occasional independent observations by staff.

During baseline (see Figure 6.8), there was a mean of 14.6 worried statements per day, 50% of which Mrs. Brooks responded to with praise or some form of attention. The analysis of the antecedent events to the state-

FIGURE 6.7. Verbal behavior record: Mr. Brooks

Date: *Wednesday, December 14*

Time		What Happened Before?	What did he say?			How did you respond?			
Start	Stop		Worried Statement	Positive Statement	Appropriate Initiation	Praise	Ignore	Punished	Other (Explain)
noon	1:15	Finished lunch	It's so dark in this room (9 times)						I have all the lights on
1:30	1:45		Re: Doris and her former husband				x		
7:00		Wake him for dinner	It is too dark in this house						All the lights are on
8:00	9:00	Watching baseball on TV		Parks we visited in other cities		x			
1:00	1:10		Do I have money in the bank? (3 times)						Gave total

FIGURE 6.8. Mr. Brooks' frequency of positive and worried statements per day

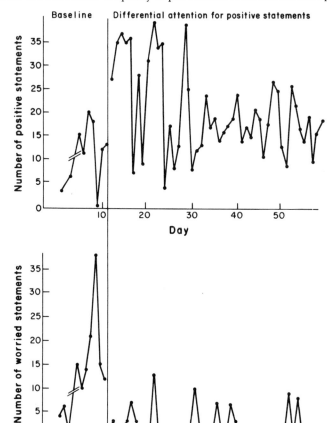

ments revealed that 93% of the statements were preceded by withdrawal of Mrs. Brooks's attention or presence from Mr. Brooks (e.g., preparing to run an errand, cooking, talking on the telephone). Mr. Brooks spoke positively on an average of 10.3 times per day, 76% of which his wife responded to with praise or attention.

The Brooks both desired an increase of positive statements of their behavioral objective. They agreed to work toward this goal. Differential attention was selected as the means to alter the consequences that Mrs. Brooks provided to Mr. Brooks' talking. She was instructed both orally and in writing to ignore all worried statements and to praise or attend to all positive statements. Both ignoring and praise were practiced in role play by Mrs. Brooks and the practitioner.

During the differential attention phase, notable improvements occurred in Mr. Brooks' behaviors, particularly in conversation with his wife. His worried statements were reduced from a mean of 15 statements per day to an average only 2 statements per day. His positive statements increased from an average of 10 per day to 24. Her attention to his worried statements decreased from 48% to 30%; her attention to positive and neutral statements increased from 76% to 95%.

To assess generalized effects, Mrs. Brooks completed the Zarit Family Burden Scale before and after the intervention occurred. Her score dropped from 91 to 78 of a possible 140 points, indicating a reported decrease in burden.

In this example, negative verbalizations were effectively reduced to more manageable levels, even with a severely impaired Alzheimer's patient. These procedures facilitated continuing home care for an 8-month period until his death.

IMPROVING MULTIPLE PROBLEMS

The previous examples illustrate the use of specific behavioral problems solving strategies with discrete problems. Although this presentation illustrates methods used to approach individual problem behaviors, most families present an array of difficulties requiring attention. As noted in chapters 3 and 4, problem selection is an important goal to most families, and general problems are addressed sequentially using problem severity, likelihood of change, and the educational potential of the family as selection criteria. Often the solution of one behavior problem facilitates the solution of others, either because the problems are related or because families are able to transfer their knowledge across behaviors.

Two multiple-problem cases that achieved successful outcomes are presented. In these cases, a multicomponent approach was used to change the environment, educate the caregivers, and introduce interventions in gradual overlapping fashion to facilitate learning and evaluation. The cases both involved older couples, in which the wives provided assistance for their husbands. Both husbands were more intact intellectually than the clients in the previous illustrations. Mr. Walters was more receptive to change efforts and became substantially engaged in his program. Mr. Keller, however, was much less cooperative, even though the practitioner attempted to engage him at each step of the procedure. Therefore, interventions had to be more indirect in nature.

Practice Illustration 5:
Improving Family Interaction
and Personal Care for
an Elderly Depressed Man
Practitioner/Researcher:
Rosemary Nelson Young

Mr. Keller was a 66-year-old retired factory worker who lived with his wife and two daughters in the small house where they had resided for 25 years. He was referred to the Elderly Support Project from a geriatric psychiatry inpatient unit. He was diagnosed as clinically depressed. Mr. Keller continued to be very isolated in the hospital and refused to participate in any activities after the first week. He was treated with haloperidol (Haldol) because of agitation, which occurred once or twice in the hospital. After initially visiting Mr. Keller in the hospital to explore his problems and secure consent for participation, the practitioner began a series of home visits after his discharge.

Mrs. Keller complained that her husband would not socialize or converse with family or friends. He remained in his bedroom day and night, coming out only for meals and to take his medication. He refused to bathe or wash himself. He often responded aggressively to the family's attempts to engage him in conversation, by telling them to shut up, shoving them away, or hitting them. Mrs. Keller reported that he responded in an aggressive manner when she asked him to take a bath. According to the family, they responded to his aggression by arguing back or pushing him away.

Observations made by the practitioner and an impartial observer confirmed that Mr. Keller remained in his room and responded in a hostile fashion to efforts to engage him. The observer also noticed that when his wife went downstairs, Mr. Keller came out of his room to look out the window. Four occurrences of verbal aggression occurred during the 1-hour observation. Observations also confirmed that Mr. Keller received considerable social attention while he was in the bedroom. His family entered the room to tell him about telephone calls and family news and to ask him to perform personal care tasks.

The practitioner concluded that there were at least two behavior excesses to consider—Mr. Keller's time in the bedroom and related contact with family members during that time and his aggression. Behavior deficits were also identified: personal care, especially grooming and bathing; household chores and activities; and socializing. These were discussed with the family. Their major concern was his lack of personal care activities. He had been hospitalized because he refused to bathe or engage in personal grooming. They found his refusal to care for himself and the associated side effects (body odor, possible skin problems, unkept beard, and soiled clothes) extremely objectionable and felt this was a behavior that should be changed.

Mrs. Keller and her daughters agreed to record behavior frequencies on the Daily Activity Record, noting occurrence of each of several behaviors each hour and the family's response (ignoring, praising, or criticizing). Monitored behaviors included conversation, time spent in bed, trips out of the house, personal care, household chores, socializing, stepping out of the bedroom, and others (including physical aggressiveness). The behaviors were defined, and recording was practiced with the family. Observer reliability checks confirmed that the family developed accurate recording skills.

Intervention 1: Personal Care. Eight days of preliminary recording indicated that Mr. Keller's level of personal care was limited to one instance of combing his hair. A procedure was developed to gradually increase Mr. Keller's personal hygiene. For the first 2 days, Mrs. Keller was instructed to approach her husband after he awakened and, while he was still in bed, to wash his face and hands with a warm wet washcloth and dry them with a towel. While doing so she was to speak in a soft voice about pleasant subjects or not talk at all. After washing his face and hands, she was to bring him a cup of coffee or tea and to offer to prepare his breakfast.

From Day 3 to Day 10, Mrs. Keller was to place a small bowl of warm water on the bedside table and use it to rinse the washcloth. She was to continue the washing procedure during this time. The purpose of this phase was to introduce bathing to Mr. Keller and to desensitize his possible anxiety or fears about bathing.

On Day 10 Mrs. Keller was to ask Mr. Keller to take a bath after she completed the washing procedure. She should tell him that breakfast would be ready after his bath and what would be served. She was to repeat this cue once or twice, but not more than two times. If Mr. Keller became angry or hostile, she was to leave the room and not return for 5 minutes. On Day 20 Mrs. Keller was to begin a maintenance procedure where she no longer washed him but continued the cueing for bathing.

Findings from personal care interventions showed that, during preintervention baseline, Mr. Keller engaged in only one personal care activity, or an average of .12 per day. During Intervention Phase 1, when washing was introduced, personal care activities increased to one occurrence each day. During Intervention Phase 2, when the washing continued, personal care occurred on a daily average of 1.3 instances each day, and Mr. Keller took one bath during the first week. During the maintenance phase, when Mrs. Keller no longer washed her husband, but continued to cue him, he maintained his personal care at a level of 1.2 occurrences per day. During this time he began to wash his face and hands when he used the washroom (see Figure 6.9a).

Notable improvement had occurred in Mr. Keller's personal care, particularly considering the near-zero initial level. The Kellers, although not fully satisfied with his self-care levels, were able to continue caring for him over 6 months, while behavioral recording continued, and they have been able to maintain him at home for over a year. They have occasionally sought some outside help for major personal care tasks (haircutting, bathing), but he has been able to continue his daily hygiene on an ongoing basis.

Intervention 2: Aggression and Socialization. Both the family and the practitioner were concerned about Mr. Keller's physical aggression. During the

FIGURE 6.9. Mr. Keller's multi-intervention program

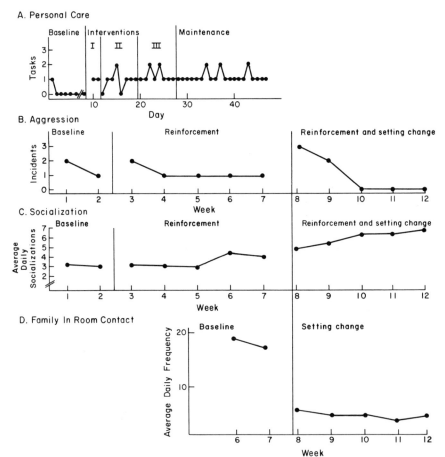

period when personal care activities were being monitored and first intervened upon, aggression was also monitored. The Kellers reported that aggression had occurred four times during the previous 2 weeks. In addition Mr. Keller's positive or neutral contacts (socializing) with others were monitored. An average of 3.3 of these socialization periods occurred each day during this phase.

The practitioner instructed Mrs. Keller and her daughters in the use of differential attention. Mr. Keller's family agreed to praise positive behaviors, such as presence in a room other than the bedroom, appropriate conversation, improvements in physical appearance, and other activities. The family agreed to ignore any aggressive behavior on his part. They discussed their use of criticism and the problems in using it as a method to manage behavior. They agreed to record when they criticized Mr. Keller without specific plans for such criticism.

With the use of this intervention, there was a decrease in aggression and an increase in socialization. Aggression decreased from an average of one occurrence every 3 days to one every 5 days. Socialization increased minimally from an average of 3.3 occurrences per day to about 3.7 per day (Figure 6.9b,c). This intervention overlapped considerably with the personal care interventions described previously. Physical aggression decreased around the time that Mrs. Keller began to wash her husband's face. Personal care continued to improve as the Kellers learned differential attention procedures. It appears that the combination of the two kinds of procedures enhanced both interventions.

Intervention 3: Increasing Household Chores. One of the behaviors the Kellers learned to praise was Mr. Keller's performance of household activities. During the first 13-day baseline period Mr. Keller did 10 household activities, such as picking up objects or taking out the garbage. During the period following the introduction of differential attention, Mr. Keller did six household chores, an increase from an average of .8 per day to one per day. A nonverbal cueing procedure was then introduced. Mrs. Keller noticed that one day, when she left the garbage on a kitchen chair near the door, he took it out. Mrs. Keller agreed to leave garbage to be taken out on the chair and Mr. Keller's jacket hanging on the door handle nearby. No verbal cue was provided by the practitioner, and the family reportedly did not prompt Mr. Keller.

During this phase, Mr. Keller completed 32 household tasks in 27 days, representing an average of 8 tasks per week. This compares very favorably with the preintervention baseline of between five and six tasks a week. Although the difference is not dramatic, it represents a regular, daily, out-of-bed activity for Mr. Keller that contributed to the overall well-being of the family. It also supported the need to look for other than verbal methods to deal with his problem behaviors.

Intervention 4: Reducing Intrusive Family Contacts. The Keller family still were not satisfied with the quality of their interaction with Mr. Keller. In particular they desired that he spend less time in bed or in his room. In assessing family activities the practitioner noted that family members frequently entered Mr. Keller's room, asked him questions, reported information to him, and demanded that he engage in particular activities. Further exploration of this situation with Mrs. Keller revealed that, although Mrs. Keller had moved out of the room several years ago, she kept many of her possessions in the room. They included both personal items and cooking supplies. It appeared that the environment was set up to foster continuing interaction between Mr. Keller and his family, possibly at a level in excess of his needs. In fact, the family was bothering Mr. Keller and denying him a satisfying level of privacy.

To document the family interaction, the Kellers agreed to keep a record of in-bedroom contact. A recording log was hung on the door, and the family noted any time a person walked into the bedroom (stepped over the threshold). The frequency of family trips into his room was graphed and is presented in Figure 6.9d. During this baseline period the family entered the room an average of 18 times a day, and the highest number of occurrences was 27 times in one day.

To increase the amount of time Mr. Keller spent out of bed, family members were instructed to refrain from entering Mr. Keller's bedroom or speaking to him while he was in bed. In order to accomplish this, several items were removed from the room, to diminish the need for the family to enter the room. These included a laundry hamper and a chest of drawers containing frequently used items such as cleaning and office supplies. The intervention to reduce negative family interaction consisted of differential attention (not attending to Mr. Keller while he was in bed) and environmental restructuring to remove cues for excessive family contact.

The in-room contacts were reviewed in weekly meetings. During intervention, family in-room contacts decreased from an average of 18 per day before intervention to an average of 3 per day when household objects were removed and the family was instructed to remain outside the room.

In addition Mr. Keller's socializing behavior improved. During the pre-intervention period this occurred at an average of 3.3 times a day. Following the reduction of in-room contacts this increased to 5.7 (see Figure 6.9c). A reversal design was used to evaluate the effects of the intervention. During the reversal the family partially increased their in-bedroom time. No materials were returned to the room. Mr. Keller's socializing, however, continued to maintain during this phase. These data suggest the difficulties in evaluating multiple interventions. Possibly the continuing increases in socializing could be accounted for by other preintervention behavior levels of entering the bedroom, so a real evaluation cannot be made.

It is noted that during this intervention Mr. Keller refused his medication on six occasions. In later maintenance phases he refused his medication (Haldol) more regularly. The change in the medication may have contributed to his behavioral changes.

During the maintenance phase Mrs. Keller continued to use the intervention procedures. She used a weekly checklist to monitor the frequency of target behaviors and then compared this information to a goal rate previously established during treatment. In this way Mrs. Keller and her daughters could systematically increase or decrease their attention to particular behaviors, based on the data. This checklist demanded much less time and attention from the family than previous data collection procedures because of its once-a-week nature.

In this case the Kellers' knowledge of behavioral principles and, in particular, their use of positive attention allowed them to maintain Mr. Keller at home. A multiple-replication design (Pinkston et al., 1982) was used to evaluate the impact that contracts made on the family. Their application of the principles was impressive because Mr. Keller was uncooperative and made family participation in the program difficult. It is also noteworthy that, as Mr. Keller's behavior improved, Mrs. Keller became more active outside of the home. She started taking driving lessons, made a 3-day visit to her daughter who lived out of town, and was even considering a part-time job.

Practice Illustration 6:
Reducing Reported Hallucinations
and Improving Activities
Practitioner/Researcher: Judy N. Jacobi

Mr. Walters, a 61-year-old, formerly self-employed man, had been forced to retire as a Social Security disability recipient because of chronic illness. Over the last decade, he had experienced numerous hospitalizations for gall bladder surgery, open-heart surgery, diabetes, and, most recently, the diagnosis of Parkinson's disease and the mild dementia related to both Parkinson's and arteriosclerosis. He took six medications daily including insulin.

An initial interview with Mr. Walters revealed a physically frail man of limited mobility who clearly enjoyed the opportunity to talk with the practitioner. He took a large measure of pride in his past successful military career and varied employment history—as a tavern and grocery store owner and, at one time, as a "million dollar round table" life insurance salesman. He previously pursued many interests, including spectator sports and cross-country travel, and regularly attended church and meetings of civic organizations in which he held office.

He had outlived two wives and was married to his third, a physically healthy 61-year-old woman. She had been referred by the Visiting Nurse Association to a practitioner at a senior center that specialized in mental health services for help with numerous problems with Mr. Walters. At the point of referral, Mrs. Walters was strongly considering nursing home placement. She was physically exhausted, emotionally distraught, and willing to try anything. Her description of presenting problems included a wide range of areas: very infrequent compliance with self-dressing and self-hygiene, lack of physical activity of any kind including nonadherence to a physician-recommended daily exercise regimen, poor speech enunciation, incontinence, excessive salivation, excessive demands about food preference and sloppiness at mealtime, and daily periods of hallucinatory activity. Mrs. Walters stated that she was doing everything for Mr. Walters, and he was acting nasty all the time.

The Walters lived in a rural setting. Mrs. Walters was the primary caregiver, although her daughter (who was 8-months pregnant at the time) and son-in-law lived with them. During the initial assessment, the practitioner administered structured assessment tools for both Mr. and Mrs. Walters. Although one of the major problems presented was noncompliance with self-dressing and self-care, on the day of the first meeting with the practitioner, Mr. Walters got out of bed himself and bathed and dressed himself, albeit with some difficulty. Mrs. Walters reported ''He looked forward to meeting all week.'' Target behaviors identified were

- Increased compliance with self-dressing and self-hygiene
- Reduced saliva output, which created a mess everywhere the client stood or ate
- Adequately anticipated toileting needs, to reduce urinary accidents
- Increased in-home physical activity, whether in terms of exercise regimen or mobility in general, such as walking with a walker several times a day
- Reduced demands about food preference, which lead to arguments
- Reduced sloppiness at the table at mealtime, defined as food dropping out of the mouth and not being recovered
- Reduced hallucinations, which were extremely disturbing to the client and disruptive to the family
- Increased better enunciation of speech, so that family members could understand the client
- Improved general attitude including decreased argumentative speech and increased pleasant speech toward the wife.

To provide baseline data, Mrs. Walters completed a Daily Activities Checklist, which gave an overview of nonoccurrence and occurrence of behaviors and familial response to them (see Figure 6.10), and a family behavior record, which focused on specific behaviors in terms of antece-

FIGURE 6.10. Mr. Walters' daily activities

ACTIVITY HOW DONE FAMILY RESPONSE

	NOT AT ALL	WITH HELP	WHEN ASKED	INDEPENDENTLY	DIDN'T NOTICE	IGNORED	ASKED TO DO SOMETHING	PRAISED	OTHER
DRESSING									
Stockings		x				x		x	Will dress only on request. Told how nice he looks when dressed.
Shoes		x				x		x	
Tie and Shoes	x					x			
Underwear		x				x			
Zipper				x					
Buttoning		x		x					
EATING									
Fork and spoon		x		x					Little sign of table manners.
Cutting		x							
Drinking				x					
HYGIENE									
Wash face			x			x		x	Bathe and shave only on request.
Comb hair			x			x		x	
Shave		x	x			x		x	
Bathe/shower				x		x		x	
Brush teeth		x				x		x	
HOUSEKEEPING									
Make Bed									
Sweep/Vacuum									
Set table									
Make coffee			x					x	
Cook									

(continued)

FIGURE 6.10. (*continued*)

ACTIVITY   HOW DONE   FAMILY RESPONSE

	NOT AT ALL	WITH HELP	WHEN ASKED	INDEPENDENTLY	DIDN'T NOTICE	IGNORED	ASKED TO DO SOMETHING	PRAISED	OTHER
ACTIVITY									
Play cards									Lost interest in most recreation or walking.
Watch TV					x				
Read					x				
Write ins:									
COMMUNICATION									
Answer phone					x				Won't answer door out of fear/ hallucinations.
Answer door									
Write									
Converse					x				

dents, behaviors, and consequences. Mrs. Walters' compliance with the latter tool was somewhat limited due to excessive demands and stress. The practitioner and Mrs. Walters arranged brief meetings away from home, which allowed the practitioner better access to information and, more importantly, enabled Mrs. Walters to get some much needed respite, which she enjoyed. This also gave the practitioner the opportunity to reinforce her.

In order to involve Mr. Walters in the concrete intervention experience, the practitioner designed and gave him a simple daily behavior self-recording instrument. This allowed the practitioner to assess Mr. Walters' ability to perform self-recording functions. On this instrument, he was asked to check whether he was feeling "nasty" or "nice" each day after breakfast. For one week he recorded that he felt nice five days and felt nasty one day. On the other day he wrote, "½ and ½," explaining in the interview that he felt half nice and half nasty that day.

The practitioner checked reliability through phone conversations with different family members and was satisfied with the consistency of the information. She was, however, unable to observe any of Mr. Walters' hallucinatory behavior and was forced to rely on his and his wife's data, which indicated an average of six occurrences in a 24-hour period.

During weekly meetings, Mr. Walters was given a series of task assignment contracts addressing daily exercise, self-dressing, and self-hygiene. These were written and placed on the refrigerator door. A written self-recording tool for compliance and noncompliance with the contract terms was left with Mr. Walters in his den. (Mr. Walters enjoyed entering into contracts—as a life insurance salesman, he had had many people sign their names on dotted lines.) These contracts were reviewed and reformulated as necessary during each weekly meeting.

Practitioner and family praise were extended in accordance with trends shown in the reviews of the self-recording tools. In formulating the contract for self-dressing, for example, walking through the motions of dressing gave Mrs. Walters insight into some of the barriers that Mr. Walters sometimes experienced, such as periodic confusion when faced with choices and the need to select what to wear. A simplified incremental approach was taught in this case. Reformulating the contracts was necessary because there were some days when Mr. Walters simply did not feel well enough to attempt the activities. Mrs. Walters was taught to approach this in as positive a manner as she could, so as not to foster dependence. During the contracting periods (14 days) Mr. Walters complied one half of the time with self-dressing and self-hygiene skills. He gave the physician-prescribed exercise regimen a try but only succeeded two times in a 2-week period. It was simply too much of an ordeal for the whole family. Since he had begun making more frequent visits to the bathroom according to a toileting schedule—every hour and a quarter—the practitioner and the family agreed that, in fact, he was getting some exercise. His family was quite satisfied with this outcome, because his condition was really quite poor at this time.

At the same time as all of these things were being done, the practitioner also began to deal with the hallucinatory behavior. After discussion of the etiology of the hallucinations with Mr. Walters' physician, relaxation exercises were taught to the client to counter stress, which was associated with the onset of these hallucinations. He and his family were also taught redirection strategies. These techniques consisted of the client's blinking his eyes repeatedly and looking in another direction when it was evident that the client was slipping into a hallucinatory pattern. He was to do this himself if he could, and both his wife and stepdaughter were to cue him with the words ''Blink it away'' if they observed the pattern. The cue was to be followed by engagement in something else, be it conversation or activity of some sort. This seemed to cut off the hallucinations, if not prevent them. Finally, contracting not to report occurrence daily was tried. The process of relaxation, redirection, and contracting for not reporting the hallucinations was done incrementally over 2 weeks' time and was very successful.

The family was taught that regular inclusion in conversation helped decrease salivation. Eliciting even a one- or two-word response triggered the swallowing mechanism and reduced the reservoir of saliva somewhat, so that it dripped less. The more he was talked to, the less mumbling seemed to be a problem, especially when eye contact and touch were extended. Food dropping was addressed with the help of a good blender. Mr. Walters was very concerned about weight loss, and he didn't have a strong preference about the form of the food as it entered his mouth. Mrs. Walters was also instructed not to sit directly across from him and observe his every bite, as this made him self-conscious and increased his food dropping. Mrs. Walters was also instructed to ignore the food preference demands.

After this initial and very successful intervention period, Mr. Walters was hospitalized for 11 days for evaluation following what was believed to be a stroke. When the practitioner visited him, however, she found him to be alert, his usual witty self, and not any more impaired than he had been at home. Unfortunately, while in the hospital Mr. Walters developed a serious yeast infection—which persisted after his discharge. This made it impossible for him to get dressed because clothes exacerbated the irritation. A urinary tract infection was discovered during a routine examination in the hospital and treated, thus taking care of the incontinence.

Mr. Walters displayed multiple behavioral excesses and deficits that lent themselves well to a structured behavioral approach. The approach enabled the family to enter into the process as participants. This was enhanced by the desire of each member to articulate the problems and frustrations openly. Although Mr. Walters was very impaired physically, he demonstrated exceptional emotional and mental resources, which, once recognized by the family, helped them to view him less as a dependent and more as a person.

Following intervention and Mr. Walters' hospitalization, the Walters sold their rural home and moved into a subsidized apartment for handicapped persons. Although the move was difficult for them, Mrs. Walters continued to utilize to the best of her ability what she had learned during the 11-week intervention period.

In summary, Mr. and Mrs. Walters have been able to solve most of his behavioral problems and have successfully lived in this improved community setting for many months.

Chapter 7
Summary: The Model and Its Uses

The procedures used in the model described in this book are successful for modifying behaviors of the elderly through behavioral family intervention. These modifications are categorized as increasing desirable activities and remediating or decreasing problematic behaviors, monitoring and feedback, goal setting, and environmental changes leading to behavioral improvements. Examples of behavioral improvement include social activities, decreased negative behaviors, self-care activities, social interactions, and planning for life changes such as a move to a new apartment. An associated side effect of behavior change is frequently an improvement in memory abilities, in most cases to more normal ranges. A substantial range of behaviors characterized as depressed, organically impaired, or psychotic respond to behavioral interventions.

Family members learn to provide adequate support for the maintenance of older persons at home. Operationally defining and quantifying behaviors offers caregivers information regarding the trends of problem behaviors and aids in decisions about changes in caregiving practices. It also provides the means for feedback to caregivers about their technique, both for insuring more adaptive caregiver behavior and for improving the behavioral levels of clients. Caregivers attend to positive behaviors while ignoring dysfunctional behaviors. Training them to use praise results in less restrictive care practices, and teaching them to use maintenance procedures, including links to community services and systematic fading of practitioner support, increases the likelihood of continued family assistance.

Several behavioral techniques successfully promote behavioral changes in the elderly: contracting and feedback to increase activities, response opportunities and contingent praise to promote positive behaviors such as self-care, differential attention to promote higher rates of existing behaviors, activity schedules to promote appropriate toilet behaviors and medication taking, and increased general levels of reinforcement to promote higher levels of activities.

The implementation of this model promotes continued living at home as an alternative to residential long-term-care placement. Actual family caregiving varies throughout the course of intervention according to the degree of self-care and ability to change. The intervention methods outlined in chapter 4 provide the base of the model: initiation, assessment and initial contracting, baseline data collection, treatment implementation, treatment evaluation, maintenance procedures, termination and follow-up.

MODEL SUMMARY

During the initiation of the program the eligibility of the candidates is evaluated for available services and to determine whether or not they meet the client and caregiver criteria for the program and what types of medication they take. The mental and physical health of the caregivers are assessed to determine their ability to participate, and an evaluation of their motivation is conducted. The caregiver assessment is essential, and it is particularly important that elderly persons have a caregiver who is closely involved with their welfare.

The orientation of clients and caregivers increases their understanding of the way problems are conceptualized including the value of objectively defining behaviors and their consequences. Once this is accomplished, the process for defining problems and problem areas for intervention is the logical next step.

Behavioral procedures are designed to increase positive behaviors of clients and their caregivers while diminishing negative behaviors. In order to counterbalance the usual pathological or negative conceptualization of elderly clients, problems are defined as positive behaviors that need developing or reinstituting. Basic assumptions of this redefinition are drawn from previous research (Pinkston & Linsk, in press) as follows:

(a) Positive behaviors are often incompatible with noxious behaviors; therefore, an increase in positive behavior will automatically decrease the noxious behaviors that are no longer reinforced.

(b) A negative definition of behaviors may routinely lead to aversive techniques, including unnecessary medication, leaving the elderly person without the necessary repertoire for achieving naturally reinforcing consequences.

(c) Immediate definition and decrease of noxious behaviors are essential if they place the elderly client at risk of long-term placement.

Behavioral definitions enable the practitioner to design programs that include reinforcement procedures as the major focus, with cueing and stimulus controls as important additions. Following the definition of behavioral deficits and excesses, caregivers are taught to record data on the occurrence of behaviors, events surrounding the onset of those behaviors, and events following those behaviors. These data allow the client, the caregiver, and the practitioner to assess possible causal and maintenance variables for negative behaviors and the absence of supporting and maintenance variables for desirable behaviors.

Caregivers then learn to use behavioral procedures and to understand reinforcement. This includes an orientation to operant and social-learning theory, with specific examples relevant to their problems. The training procedures used are modeling, role play, corrective feedback, and discussion of the data. The interventions are reinforcement, stimulus control, and community links. These are combined in contracts among clients, caregivers, and practitioners and use specific procedures such as praise contingent on the occurrence of behaviors, prompts, scheduled activities, and differential attending.

Once improvement is attained, it is necessary, particularly with the elderly, to plan sufficient environmental consequences and stimulation to maintain the program effects. This planning begins during assessment, as behaviors that are more likely to be valued are selected for intervention. The deterioration of behavioral gains can be avoided by planned decrease of the practitioner's involvement and simultaneous increase in caregiver control of the intervention planning, along with continued used of clear antecedent cues and maintenance of consequences for behavior.

With the elderly, termination is a very gradual process and begins once stable levels of improved behavior are present. At that time responsibility for monitoring and intervention are transferred to the caregiver, and the practitioner fades control, support, and frequency of visits. All practitioner visits cease within 2 months, depending to some degree on client and caregiver needs.

EVALUATION

In this model, evaluation plays a primary role in all clinical aspects of the program and is used to guide the practitioner's decisions regarding assessment, intervention, maintenance, and follow-up. Simple single-case designs are used to evaluate ongoing patterns of behavior during baseline, to note changes that occur following intervention, and to monitor maintenance of changes. The clinical multiple-baseline design, multiple-baseline, and AB designs are most frequently useful for this purpose. Although it is difficult to claim causal relationships between variables, these designs are a step forward in decision making for the practitioner, the client, and the caregiver because they allow a better analysis of progress than subjective observations of a frail elderly person might provide. As important as the discrimination of change is the discrimination of the absence of change; the absence of the necessary components of change, such as the failure of the caregiver to implement the procedures; and the absence of available reinforcers.

In order to use single-case designs, time-series data in the form of direct observation of frequency, duration, or latency of behaviors are required. Pre and post measures are also helpful, but some form of time-series data is essential in making clinical decisions. Two types of data are used most frequently, time sampling and checklists. When the time-sampling technique is used, the observer records the occurrence or nonoccurrence of behaviors during specific times. Checklists are used to record occurrences of behavior during a particular time period, usually a long period, such as the number of trips out of the house during the day, for instance, from 7 a.m. to 7 p.m. The client's problem and the circumstances surrounding it are used to decide the method of data recording and the caregiver's ability to record.

Pre and post questionnaires are administered to ascertain the client's overall well-being before and after intervention and the caregiver's and client's satisfaction regarding the fit between the program and their needs. Changes in responses between pre and post questionnaires are unlikely except in areas that are chosen for intervention; an exception is the Mental Status Questionnaire. In the Elderly Support Project, studies on the improvement on this instrument are correlated with positive changes in behaviors such as increased activity and verbal skills.

Analysis of the findings of the research evaluating this program indicated maintenance or improvement in behavior in 78% of behaviors chosen for intervention. Reinforcement, contracting, and stimulus cues comprised the primary intervention procedures. Increasing desirable behavior was the focus of 76% of the interventions, including such behaviors as self-care and social activities. No punishment procedures were used. The average percentage of improvement on mental status scores was approximately 15% between pre and post assessment. Although there were general reports of improvement by clients and caregivers, the largest improvements were increased frequency of home activities and independent abilities (Pinkston & Linsk, in press).

These findings show that behavioral family-training procedures have utility when working with the impaired elderly and their families. The improvement of environmental consequences can defer or eliminate the need for institutional placement. These methods provide specific training methods for practitioners to use effectively with family caregivers.

ROLE AND SETTING CONSIDERATIONS

Because this model is not yet widely used with the elderly, the practitioner may be the agency authority on behavior analysis or behavior modification. And, if the methods work for the practitioner, there may be interest shown by other professionals in these procedures. It should be assumed that this interest means that others are eager to learn behavioral techniques. Because of the practical and helpful interventions, it is unlikely that supervisors will discourage their use. There may, however, be a wait-and-see attitude, and the practitioner should be wary of referral of all of the cases for whom nothing has worked. Although behaviorism has cut its teeth on such cases, it may be discouraging for a person just learning to use the procedures. If professional colleagues show interest in the procedures the practitioner is using, it is only reasonable that they should be shared and a structure should be provided in the form of regular meetings to avoid drive-in consultation in the halls. Procedures have been defined for consulting with colleagues (see Pinkston et al., 1982, chap. 8). A good beginning, however, is to invite outside discussion on this model or on behavioral interventions in general, to lay the groundwork for the practitioner's new role as consultant. As with all other important problem solving, arrange a formal time and place for any advice you have to give, and try to avoid showing disappointment if interventions don't work out as expected.

SUMMARY

Behavioral methods have relevance for other populations and problems, and the behavioral family treatment model is particularly important for families with stresses brought on by clients with handicaps requiring special care. The delivery of this program will vary depending on the skill levels of the caregivers, the specific problems involved, and the need for concrete supports. There are procedures within the model that are of value to caregivers of people with chronic mental and physical illness as well as lesser problems. Behavioral procedures have great utility for problems associated with aging such as depressions, family conflicts, and increasing activities. Behavioral interventions can be used to prevent further deterioration and to regenerate activity levels in those recovering from illness.

For most people, the family is the basic unit of support, and, for the disabled, the family is the most frequent care provider. This behavioral family model can help caregivers support clients in positive and systematic ways by emphasizing and enhancing their positive characteristics and behaviors in an environment in which there are consistent consequences for positive behaviors of both clients and caregivers.

Bibliography

SELF-CARE BEHAVIORS

Eating

Baltes, M. M., & Lascomb, S. L. (1975). Creating a healthy institutional environment for the elderly via behavior management: The nurse as a change agent. *International Journal of Nursing Studies, 12,* 5–12.

Blackman, D. K., Gehle, C., & Pinkston, E. M. (1979). Reestablishment of appropriate utensil use among the institutionalized elderly. *Social Work Research and Abstracts, 15,* 18–24.

Edwards, K. A. (1979). Dining experience in the institutionalized setting. *Nursing Homes, 28,* 6–17.

Geiger, O. G., & Johnson, L. A. (1974). Positive education for elderly persons: Correct eating through reinforcement. *The Gerontologist, 14,* 432–436.

Incontinence

Atthowe, J. (1972). Controlling nocturnal enuresis in severely disabled and chronic patients. *Behavior Therapy, 3,* 232–239.

Blackman, D. K. (1977, December). *Control of urinary incontinence among institutionalized elderly.* Paper presented at the 11th Annual Convention of the Association for Advancement of Behavior Therapy, Atlanta.

Collins, R., & Plaska, T. (1975). Mowrer's conditioning treatment for enuresis applied to residents of a nursing home. *Behavior Therapy, 6,* 632–638.

Grosicki, J. P. (1968). Effects of operant conditioning on modification of incontinence in neuro-psychiatric geriatric patients. *Nursing Research, 17,* 304–311.

Howe, M. W. (1975). *Behavior management of urinary incontinence in the elderly.* Unpublished doctoral dissertation, The University of Chicago, School of Social Service Administration.

Pollack, D. D., & Lieberman, R. P. (1974). Behavior therapy of incontinence in demented inpatients. *The Gerontologist, 14,* 488–491.

Young, R. N., Linsk, N. L., Pinkston, E. M., & Green, G. R. (1983, May 27). *Behavioral treatment of incontinence in the elderly: Adapting institutional procedures to home-based family settings.* Poster presented at the Association for Behavior Analysis Annual Meeting, Milwaukee.

Ambulation Problems

DiScipio, W., & Feldman, M. (1971). Combined behavior therapy and physical therapy in the treatment of a fear of walking. *Journal of Behavior Therapy and Experimental Psychiatry, 2,* 151–152.

Koncelik, J. A., & Snyder, L. (1971). The role of design in behavioral manipulation within long-term care facilities. *Nursing Homes, 20,* 2–23.

Libb, J. W., & Clements, C. (1969). Tokens in an exercise program for hospitalized geriatric patients. *Perceptual and Motor Skills, 28,* 957–958.

MacDonald, M. L., & Butler, A. K. (1974). Reversal of helplessness: Producing walking behavior in nursing home wheelchair residents using behavior modification procedures. *Journal of Gerontology, 29,* 97–101.

Proppe, H. (1968). Housing for the retired and aged in southern California: An architectural commentary. *The Gerontologist, 8,* 176–179.

Other Personal Care

Haynes, S. N., Prince, M. G., & Simmons, J. B. (1975). Stimulus control treatment of insomnia. *Journal of Behavior Therapy and Experimental Psychiatry, 6,* 279–282.

Rinke, C. L., Williams, J. J., Lloyd, K. E., & Smith-Scott, W. (1978). The effects of prompting and reinforcement on self-bathing by elderly residents of a nursing home. *Behavior Therapy, 9,* 873–881.

Sachs, D. A. (1975). Behavioral techniques in a residential nursing home facility. *Journal of Behavior Therapy and Experimental Psychiatry, 6,* 123–127.

Schwartz, A., & Blackman, D. K. (1976). Re-establishment of self-dressing. *Developing behavior therapies for the institutionalized elderly* (pp. 91–98). Project report submitted to Illinois Department of Mental Health and Developmental Disabilities, The University of Chicago, School of Social Service Administration, Chicago.

NEGATIVE BEHAVIORS

Self-injurious Behaviors

Mishara, B. L., Robertson, B., & Kastenbaum, R. (1974). Self-injurious behavior in the elderly. *The Gerontologist, 14,* 273–280.

Repetitive Movements

Albanese H., & Gaarder, K. (1977). Biofeedback treatment of tardive dyskinesia: Two case reports. *American Journal of Psychiatry, 134,* 1149–1150.

Cuvo, A. J. (1976). Decreasing repetitive behavior in an institutionalized mentally retarded resident. *Mental Retardation, 15,* 22–25.

Jackson, G. M. (1980, February). *The behavior treatment of orafacial tardive dyskinesia.* Paper presented at the First Conference on Behavior Gerontology, Nova University.

Longin, H. E., Kohn, J. P., & Macurik, K. M. (1974). The modification of choreal movements. *Journal of Behavior Therapy and Experimental Psychiatry, 5,* 263–265.

Taylor, C. B., Zlotnick, S. I., & Hoelhe, A. (1979). The effects of behavioral procedures on tardive dyskinesas. *Behavior Therapy, 10,* 37–45.

INCREASING POSITIVE BEHAVIORS

Medical Regimens

Dapcich-Miura, E., & Hovell, M. F. (1979). Contingency management of adherence to a complex medical regimen in an elderly heart patient. *Behavior Therapy, 2*, 193-201.

Increasing Physical Exercise

Adams, G. N., & deVries, H. A. (1973). Physiological effects of an exercise training regimen upon women aged 52 & 79. *Journal of Gerontology, 28*, 50-55.

Frekany, G. A., & Leslie, D. K. (1975). Effects of an exercise program on selected flexibility measures of senior citizens. *The Gerontologist, 15*, 182-193.

Libb, J. W., & Clements, C. (1969). Tokens in an exercise program for hospitalized geriatric patients. *Perceptual and Motor Skills, 28*, 957-958.

Stamford, B. A. (1972). Physiological effects of training upon institutionalized men. *Journal of Gerontology, 27*, 451-455.

Group Activity Programs

Blackman, D. K., Howe, M., & Pinkston, E. M. (1976). Increasing participation in social interaction of the institutionalized elderly. *The Gerontologist, 17*, 69-76.

Hoyer, W. J., Kafer, R. A., Simpson, S. C., & Hoyer, F. W. (1974). A reinstatement of verbal behavior in elderly mental patients using operant procedures. *The Gerontologist, 14*, 149-152.

Linsk, N. L. (1978, November). *Increasing social involvement of impaired residents of a home for the aged using outdoor day camp activities.* Paper presented at the 31st Annual Scientific Meeting of the Gerontological Society of America, Dallas.

Linsk, N. L., Howe, M. W., & Pinkston, E. (1975). Behavioral group work in a home for the aged. *Social Work, 20*, 454-463.

MacDonald, M. L., & Settin, J. M. (1978). Reality orientation versus sheltered workshops as treatment for the institutionalized aging. *Journal of Gerontology, 33*, 416-421.

McClannahan, L. E. (1973). Recreation programs for nursing home residents: The importance of patient characteristics and environmental arrangements. *Therapeutic Recreation Journal*, second quarter, 26-31.

McClannahan, L. E., & Risley, T. R. (1974). Designs of living environments for nursing home residents: Recruiting attendance in activities. *The Gerontologist, 14*, 236-240.

Mueller, D. J., & Atlas, L. (1972). Resocialization of regressed elderly patients: A behavior management approach. *Journal of Gerontology, 27*, 390-392.

Pierce, C. H. (1975). Recreation for the elderly: Activity participation at a senior citizen center. *The Gerontologist, 15*, 202-205.

Improving Verbal Behavior

Baltes, M. M., & Lascomb, S. L. (1975). Creating a healthy institutional environment for the elderly via behavior management: The nurse as a change agent. *International Journal of Nursing Studies, 12*, 5-12.

Bardin-Ayers, S. K., Potter, R. E., & McDearmon, J. R. (1975). Using reinforcement therapy and precision techniques with adult aphasics. *Journal of Behavior Therapy and Experimental Psychiatry, 6*, 301-305.

Clark, F., Miller, L. R., Thomas, J. A., Kucherawy, D. A., & Azen, S. P. (1978). A comparison of operant and sensory integrative methods on development of parameters in profoundly retarded adults. *American Journal of Occupational Therapy, 32,* 86–92.

Green, G. R., Linsk, N. L., & Pinkston, E. (1980, May). *Modification of dysfunctional verbal interactions in the elderly.* Paper presented at the meeting of the Association for Behavior Analysis, Dearborn, MI.

Green, G. R. (1982). *Modification of verbal behavior of the impaired elderly.* Unpublished doctoral dissertation, The University of Chicago, Chicago.

Hoyer, W. J., Kafer, R. A., Simpson, S. C., & Hoyer, F. W. (1974). A reinstatement of verbal behavior in elderly mental patients using operant procedures. *The Gerontologist, 14,* 149–152.

Lopez, M. A. (1978). Establishing and maintaining a social skill among elderly psychiatric patients. *Dissertation Abstracts International, 39,* 987–988.

Mueller, D. J., & Atlas, L. (1972). Resocialization of regressed elderly patients: A behavior management approach. *Journal of Gerontology, 27,* 390–392.

Sachs, D. A. (1975). Behavioral techniques in a residential nursing home facility. *Journal of Behavior Therapy and Experimental Psychiatry, 6,* 123–127.

SOCIAL BEHAVIORS

Berger, R. M., & Rose, S. D. (1977). Interpersonal skill training with institutionalized elderly patients. *Journal of Gerontology, 32,* 346–353.

Corby, M. (1975). Assertion training with aged populations. *The Counseling Psychologist, 5,* 69–74.

Edinberg, M. A., Karoly, P., & Glesler, G. (1977). Assessing assertion in the elderly: An application of the behavioral analytic model of competence. *Journal of Clinical Psychology, 33,* 869–874.

Goldstein, R. S., & Baer, D. M. (1976). R. S. V. P.: A procedure to increase the personal mail and number of correspondents for nursing home residents. *Behavior Therapy, 7,* 348–354.

Quattrochi-Tubin, S., & Jason, L. A. (1980). Enhancing social interactions and activity among the elderly through stimulus control. *Journal of Applied Behavior Analysis, 13,* 159–163.

Toseland, R. W., & Rose, S. D. (1978). Evaluating social skills training for older adults in groups. *Social Work Research and Abstracts, 14,* 25–38.

IMPROVING MEMORY

Bernstein, R., & Dvorkin, L. (November 16–20, 1978). *An alternative to reality orientation: A behavioral analytic approach.* Paper presented at the 31st Annual Scientific Meeting of the Gerontological Society of America, Dallas.

Eisdorfer, C., Cohen, D., & Preston, C. (1978, December). *Behavioral and psychological therapies for the older patient with cognitive impairment.* Paper presented at the National Institute of Health Conference on Behavioral Aspects of Senile Dementia, Washington, DC.

Taepfer, C. T., Bucknell, A. T., & Shaw, D. O. (1974). Remotivation as behavior therapy. *The Gerontologist, 14,* 451–453.

BEHAVIORAL FAMILY TRAINING
PROCEDURES

Berkowitz, B. P., & Graziano, A. M. (1972). Training parents as behavior therapists: A review. *Behaviour Research and Therapy, 10,* 297–317.

Bernal, M., Duryee, J. S., Pruett, H. I., & Burns, B. (1968). Behavior modification and the "brat syndrome." *Journal of Consulting and Clinical Psychology, 32,* 447–455.

Dangel, R. F., & Polster, R. A. (Eds.). (1983). *Parent training: Foundations of research and practice.* New York: Guilford Press.

Hawkins, R. P., Peterson, R. F., Schweid, E., and Bijou, S. W. (1966). Behavior therapy in the home: Amelioration of problem parent-child relations with the parent in a therapeutic role. *Journal of Experimental Child Psychology, 4,* 99–107.

Johnson, C. A., & Katz, R. A. (1973). Using parents as change agents for their children: A review. *Journal of Child Psychology and Psychiatry and Allied Disciplines, 14,* 181–200.

Levenstein, P., Kochman, A., & Roth, H. (1973). From laboratory to real world: Service delivery of the mother-child home program. *American Journal of Orthopsychiatry, 43,* 72–78.

O'Dell, S. (1974). Training parents in behavior modification. *Psychological Bulletin, 81,* 418–433.

O'Leary, K. D., O'Leary, S., & Becker, W. C. (1967). Modification of deviant sibling interaction patterns in the home. *Behaviour Research and Therapy, 5,* 113–120.

Patterson, G. R., Reid, J. B., Jones, R. R., & Conger, R. E. (1975). *A social learning approach to family interventions* (Vol. 1), *Families with aggressive children.* Eugene, OR: Castalia.

Pinkston, E. M., Friedman, B. S., & Polster, R. A. (1981). Educating parents as behavior change agents for their children. In S. P. Schinke (Ed.), *Behavioral modification in social work: Helping children, adults, and families in community settings.* Hawthorne, NY: Aldine.

Pinkston, E. M., & Herbert-Jackson, E. W. (1975). Modification of irrelevant and bizarre verbal behavior using mother as therapist. *Social Service Review, 49,* 46–63.

References

Albanese, H., & Gaarder, K. (1977). Biofeedback treatment of tardive dyskinesia: Two case reports. *American Journal of Psychiatry, 134,* 1149-1150.

Baer, D. M. (1973). *The analysis of behavior and the analysis of problems.* Paper presented at the fourth annual Conference on Behavior Analysis in Education, Lawrence, KS.

Baer, D. M., & Wolf, M. M. (1970). The entry into natural communities of reinforcement. In R. Ulrich, T. Stachnik, & J. Mabry (Eds.), *Control of human behavior* (Vol. 2) (pp. 319-324). Glenview, IL: Scott, Foresman.

Baer, D. M., Wolf, M. M., & Risley, T. R. (1968). Some current dimensions of applied behavior analysis. *Journal of Applied Behavior Analysis, 1,* 91-97.

Baltes, M. M., & Barton, E. M. (1977). New approaches toward aging: A case for the operant model. *Educational Gerontology, 2,* 383-405.

Baltes, M. M., & Zerbe, M. B. (1976). Independence training in nursing home residents. *The Gerontologist, 16,* 428-432.

Barney, J. L. (1977). The prerogative of choice in long-term care. *The Gerontologist, 17,* 309-314.

Bayne, J. R. D. (1971). Environmental modification for the older person. *The Gerontologist, 11,* 314-317.

Bellucci, G., & Hoyer, W. J. (1975). Feedback effects on the performance and self-reinforcing behavior of elderly and young adult women. *Journal of Gerontology, 30,* 456-460.

Bender, M. B., Fink, M., & Green, M. (1951). Patterns in perception in simultaneous tests of the face and hand. *Archives of Neurology and Psychiatry, 66,* 355-362.

Berkowitz, B. P., & Graziano, A. M. (1972). Training parents as behavior therapists: A review. *Behaviour Research and Therapy, 10,* 297-317.

Bernstein, R., & Dvorkin, L. (1978, November 16-20). *An alternative to reality orientation: A behavioral analytic approach.* Paper presented at the 31st Annual Scientific Meeting of the Gerontological Society of America, Dallas.

Bijou, S. W., Peterson, R. F., & Ault, M. H. (1968). A method to integrate descriptive and experimental field studies at the level of data and empirical concepts. *Journal of Applied Behavior Analysis, 1,* 175-191.

Blackman, D. (1981, May). *Applied behavior analysis in institutions for the elderly.* Paper presented at the 7th Annual Convention of the Association for Behavior Analysis, Milwaukee.

Blackman, D. K., Gehle, C., & Pinkston, E. M. (1979). Reestablishment of appropriate utensil use among the institutionalized elderly. *Social Work Research and Abstracts, 15,* 18-24.

Blackman, D. K., Howe, M., & Pinkston, E. M. (1976). Increasing participation in social interaction of the institutionalized elderly. *The Gerontologist, 17,* 69-76.

✓ Brandwein, B., & Postoff, R. (1977, November). *A didactic and therapeutic model of intervention in working with adult children of aged parents.* Paper presented at the 30th Annual Scientific Meeting of the Gerontological Society of America, San Francisco.

✓ Brody, E. M. (1967). Aging is a family affair. *Public Welfare, 25,* 129–140.

✓ Brody, S., Poulshock, W., & Masciocchi, C. (1978). The family caring unit: A major consideration in the long-term support system. *The Gerontologist, 18,* 556–561.

Brown, L. B. (1977). Treating problems of psychiatric outpatients. In W. J. Reid, & L. Epstein (Eds.), *Task-centered practice.* New York: Columbia University Press.

✓ Bumagin, V. E., & Hirn, K. F. (1979). *Aging is a family affair.* New York: T. Y. Crowell.

Burkhardt, J. E. (1979). Evaluating information and referral services. *The Gerontologist, 19,* 28–33.

Busse, E. W., & Pfeiffer, E. (1969). *Behavior and adaptation in late life.* Boston: Little, Brown.

Bussink, T., Van der Tak, J., & Zuga, C. S. (1976). *Sourcebook on population, 1970–1976.* Washington, DC: Population Reference Bureau.

✓ Butler, R. N., & Lewis, M. I. (1982). *Aging and mental health.* St. Louis: C. V. Mosby.

Cautela, J. (1966). Behavior therapy and geriatrics. *Journal of Genetic Psychology, 108,* 9–17.

Cautela, J. R., & Mansfield, L. (1977). A behavioral approach to geriatrics. In W. D. Gantry (Ed.), *Geropsychology: A model of training and clinical service.* Cambridge, MA: Ballinger.

✓ Cohen, S. Z., & Gans, B. M. (1978). *The other generation gap: The middle aged and their aging parents.* Chicago: Follett.

Eisdorfer, C. (1980, November). In W. Keckich (chair), *The family and Alzheimers Disease.* Discussion presented at the 33rd Annual Scientific Meeting of the Gerontological Society of America, San Diego.

Eisdorfer, C., Cohen, D., & Preston, C. (1978, December). *Behavioral and psychological therapies for the older patient with cognitive impairment.* Paper presented at the National Institute of Health Conference on Behavioral Aspects of Senile Dementia, Washington, DC.

Epstein, L. (1980). *Helping people: Task centered approach.* St. Louis: C. V. Mosby.

Fischer, J., & Gochros, H. L. (1975). *Planned behavior change: Behavior modification in social work.* New York: Free Press.

Frankel, R., & McCauley, D. C. (1977). *Backstage at Drexel Home.* Unpublished manuscript, Drexel Home, Chicago.

Frankfather, D. (1977). *The aged and the community: Managing senility and deviance.* New York: Praeger.

Frankfather, D., Smith, M. J., & Caro, F. G. (1981). *Family care of the elderly: Public initiatives and public obligations.* Lexington, MA: Lexington Books.

General Accounting Office of the United States (GAO), Comptroller General. (1977). *Report to Congress: The well-being of older people in Cleveland, Ohio.* Washington, DC: U.S. Government Printing Office.

✓ Goldfarb, A. I. (1965). Psychodynamics and the three generation family. In E. Shanas & G. Streib (Eds.), *Social structure and the family: Generational relations.* Englewood Cliffs, NJ: Prentice-Hall.

Goldiamond, I. (1974). Towards a constructional approach to social problems. *Behavioralism, 2,* 1–85.

Grad de Alarcon, J., Sainsbury, P., & Costain, W. R. (1975). Incidence of referred mental illness in Chichester and Salisbury. *Psychological Medicine, 5,* 32–54.

Green, G. R. (1982). *Modification of verbal behavior of the impaired elderly.* Unpublished doctoral dissertation, The University of Chicago, Chicago.

Green, G. R., Linsk, N. L., & Pinkston, E. M. (1980, May). *Modification of dysfunctional verbal interactions in the elderly.* Paper presented at the meeting of the Association for Behavior Analysis, Dearborn, MI.

Grosicki, J. P. (1968). Effects of 0 percent condition on modification of incontinence in neuro-psychiatric geriatric patients. *Nursing Research, 17,* 304–311.

Haley, W. E. (1983). A family-behavioral approach to the treatment of the cognitively impaired elderly. *The Gerontologist, 23,* 18–20.

Hall, R. V. (1971). *Managing behavior part 1: Behavior modification: The measurement of behavior.* Lawrence, KS: H & H Enterprises.

Herbert, E. M., Pinkston, E. M., Hayden, M., Sajwaj, T., Pinkston, S., Cordura, G., & Jackson, C. (1973). Adverse effects of differential parental attention. *Journal of Applied Behavior Analysis, 6,* 15–30.

Hersen, M., & Barlow, D. (1976). *Single case experimental designs: Strategies for studying behavior change.* New York: Pergamon Press.

Howe, M. W. (1975). *Behavior management of urinary incontinence in the elderly.* Unpublished doctoral dissertation, The University of Chicago, School of Social Service Administration, Chicago.

Hoyer, W. J. (1973). Application of operant techniques for the modification of elderly behavior. *The Gerontologist, 13,* 18–22.

Hoyer, W. J., Mishara, B. L., & Reidel, R. G. (1975). Problem behaviors as operants: Applications with elderly individuals. *The Gerontologist, 15,* 452–456.

Hoyer, W. J., Kafer, R. A., Simpson, S. C., & Hoyer, F. W. (1974). Reinstatement of verbal behavior in elderly clients using operant procedures. *The Gerontologist, 14,* 149–152.

Hudson, W. W. (1981). Development and use of indexes and scales. In R. M. Grinnell (Ed.), *Social Work Research and Evaluation.* Itasca, IL: F. E. Peacock.

Hussian, R. A. (1981). *Geriatric psychology: A behavioral perspective.* New York: Van Nostrand Reinhold.

Jackson, G. M. (1980, February). *The behavior treatment of orafacial tardive dyskinesia.* Paper presented at the first Conference on Behavior Gerontology, Nova University.

Jayaratne, S., & Levy, R. (1979). *Empirical clinical practice.* New York: Columbia University Press.

Johnson, C. A., & Katz, R. A. (1973). Using parents as change agents for their children: A review. *Journal of Child Psychology and Psychiatry and Allied Disciplines, 14,* 181–200.

Kahn, R. L., Goldfarb, A. I., Pollock, M., & Peck, R. (1960). Brief objective measures for the determination of mental status in the aged. *American Journal of Psychiatry, 117,* 326–328.

Kahn, R. S. (1965). Comments. In *Proceedings of the York House Institute on mentally impaired aged.* Philadelphia: Philadelphia Geriatric Center.

Kanfer, F., & Saslow, G. (1969). Behavioral diagnosis. In C. M. Franks (Ed.), *Behavior therapy: Appraisal and status.* New York: McGraw-Hill.

Kastenbaum, R. (1968). Perspectives on the development and modification of behavior in the aged: A developmental-field perspective. *The Gerontologist, 25,* 280–283.

Keller, J. F., & Hughston, G. A. (1981). *Counseling the elderly: A systems approach.* New York: Harper & Row.

Kirk, S. A., & Greenley, J. R. (1974). Denying or delivering services? *Social Work, 19,* 439–447.

Kleban, M. H., Brody, E. M., & Lawton, M. P. (1971). Personality traits in the mentally impaired aged and their relationship to improvement in current functioning. *The Gerontologist, 11,* 134–140.

Kosberg, J. I. (1979, November). *Family conflict and abuse of the elderly relative.* Paper presented at the 32nd Annual Scientific Meeting of the Gerontological Society, Washington, DC.

Kratochwill, T. R. (1978). *Single subject research: Strategies for evaluation of change.* New York: Academic Press.

Kulys, R., & Tobin, S. S. (1980). Older people and their responsible others. *Social Work, 25,* 138–145.

Lau, E. E., & Kosberg, J. I. (1978, November). *Abuse of the elderly by informal care providers: Practice and research issues.* Paper presented at the 31st Annual Scientific Meeting of the Gerontological Society of America, Dallas.

Levendusky, P. G. (1978). Effects of social incentives on task performance in the elderly. *Journal of Gerontology, 33,* 562–566.

Levit, G. (1978). Children of the elderly as natural helpers: Some demographic differences. *American Journal of Community Psychology, 6,* 489–498.

Lindsley, O. R. (1964). Geriatric behavioral prosthetics. In R. Kastenbaum (Ed.), *New thoughts on old age.* New York: Springer.

Linsk, N. L., Howe, M. W., & Pinkston, E. M. (1975). Behavioral group work in a home for the aged. *Social Work, 20,* 454–463.

Linsk, N. L., Pinkston, E. M., & Green, G. R. (1982). Home-based behavioral social work with the elderly. In Pinkston, E. M., Levitt, J. L., Green, G. R., Linsk, N. L., & Rzepnicki, T. L. *Effective social work practice: Advanced techniques for behavioral intervention with individuals, families and institutional staff,* San Francisco: Jossey-Bass.

MacDonald, M. L. (1978). Environmental programming for the socially isolated aged. *The Gerontologist, 18,* 350–354.

MacDonald, M. L., & Butler, A. K. (1974). Reversal of helplessness: Producing walking behavior in nursing home wheelchair residents using behavior modification procedures. *Journal of Gerontology, 29,* 97–101.

Maddox, G. L. (1975). Families as context and resource in chronic illness. In S. Sherwood (Ed.), *Long-term care: A handbook for researchers, planners, and providers.* New York: Spectrum.

McClannahan, L. E. (1973). Therapeutic and prosthetic living environments for nursing home residents. *The Gerontologist, 13,* 424–429.

McClannahan, L. E., & Risley, T. R. (1974). Designs of living environments for nursing home residents: Recruiting attendance in activities. *The Gerontologist, 14,* 236–240.

Meichenbaum, D. (1974). Self-instructional strategy training: A cognitive prosthesis for the aged. *Human Development, 17,* 273–280.

Melamed, B. G., & Siegel, L. J. (1975). Self-directed *in vivo* treatment of an obsessive compulsive checking ritual. *Journal of Behaviour Therapy and Experimental Psychiatry, 6,* 31–35.

Middleman, R., & Goldberg, G. (1974). *Social service delivery: A structured approach to social work practice.* New York: Columbia University Press.

Mishara, B. L., & Kastenbaum, R. (1973). Self-injurious behavior and environmental change in the institutional elderly. *International Journal of Aging and Human Development, 4,* 133–145.

Mishara, B. L., Robertson, B., & Kastenbaum, R. (1974). Self-injurious behavior in the elderly. *The Gerontologist, 14,* 273–280.

Morris, R. (1971). *Alternatives to nursing home care: A proposal.* Washington, DC: U.S. Government Printing Office.

Nay, W. R. (1979). Parents as real life reinforcers: The enhancement of training effects across conditions other than training. In A. P. Goldstein & F. H. Kanfer (Eds.), *Maximizing treatment gains: Transfer enhancement in psychotherapy.* New York: Academic Press.

O'Dell, S. (1974). Training parents in behavior modification. *Psychological Bulletin, 81,* 418–433.

O'Dell, S. L., O'Quin, J. A., Alford, B. A., O'Briant, A. L., & Giebenhain, J. E. (1982). Predicting the acquisition of parenting skills via four training methods. *Behavior Therapy, 13,* 194–208.

Otten, J., & Shelley, F. D. (1976). *When your parents grow older.* New York: Funk & Wagnalls.

Page, F. I. (1978). The development and evaluation of a self-management training program for older adults. *Dissertation Abstracts International, 39,* 393.

Patterson, G. R., Shaw, D. A., & Ebner, M. H. (1969). Teachers, peers, and parents as agents of change in the classroom. In F. A. M. Benson (Ed.), *Modifying deviant social behaviors in various classroom settings.* Eugene, OR: University of Oregon.

Pfeiffer, E. (1978). *Multidimensional functional assessment: The OARS methodology*. Durham, ND: Duke University Center for the Study of Aging and Human Development.

Pincus, A., & Minahan, A. (1973). *Social work practice: Model and method*. Itasca, IL: F. E. Peacock.

Pinkston, E. M. (1984). Behavioral intervention for home and school. In R. F. Dangel & R. A. Polster (Eds.), *Parent training: Foundations of research and practice*. New York: Guilford Press.

Pinkston, E. M., Budd, K., Green, G. R., & Baer, D. M. (1973). *Modeling as a technique in training parents*. Unpublished manuscript, University of Kansas, Department of Human Development, Lawrence, KS.

Pinkston, E. M., Friedman, B. S., & Polster, R. A. (1981). Parents as agents for behavior change. In S. P. Schinke (Ed.), *Behavioral methods in social welfare: Helping children, adults, and families in community settings*. New York: Aldine.

Pinkston, E. M., Levitt, J. L., Green, G. R., Linsk, N. L., & Rzepnicki, T. L. (1982). *Effective social work practice: Advanced techniques for behavioral intervention with individuals, families, and institutional staff*. San Francisco: Jossey-Bass.

Pinkston, E. M., & Linsk, N. L. (in press). Behavioral family intervention with the impaired elderly. *The Gerontologist*.

Premack, D. (1959). Toward empirical behavior laws, part 1: Positive reinforcement. *Psychological Review, 66*, 219–233.

Rankin, E. R., Linsk, N. L., & Pinkston, E. M. (1983, November). *The relationship between caregiver attitudes toward disabled elderly family members and institutional placement in a home-based behavioral treatment program*. Poster presented at the 36th Annual Scientific Meeting of the Gerontological Society of America, San Francisco.

Rapoport, R., Rapoport, R. N., & Strelitz, Z. (1970). *Fathers, mothers, and society: Towards new alliances*. New York: Basic Books.

Rathbone-McCuan, E. (1980). Elderly victims of family violence and neglect. *Social Casework, 61*, 296–304.

Rebok, G. W., & Hoyer, W. J. (1977). The functional context of elderly behavior. *The Gerontologist, 17*, 27–34.

Reid, W. J. (1978). *The task-centered system*. New York: Columbia University Press.

Reid, W. J., & Smith, A. D. (1981). *Research in social work*. New York: Columbia University Press.

Risley, T. R., & Wolf, M. M. (1972). Strategies for analyzing behavioral change over time. In J. Nesselroade & H. Reese (Eds.), *Life-span developmental psychology*. New York: Academic Press.

Safford, F. (1977). *Developing a training program for families of the mentally impaired aged*. New York: Isabella Geriatric Center.

Sager, A. (1983). A proposal for promoting more adequate long-term care of the elderly. *The Gerontologist, 23*, 13–17.

Schier, B. (1972). Closer communications through interactions in groups of aged persons. *Journal of Jewish Communal Service*, 142–166.

Schwartz, A., & Blackman, D. K. (1976). *Developing behavior therapies for the institutionalized elderly*. Project report submitted to Illinois Department of Mental Health and Developmental Disabilities, The University of Chicago, School of Social Service Administration.

Schwartz, A., & Goldiamond, I. (1975). *Social casework: A behavioral approach*. New York: Columbia University Press.

Schwartz, A. N. (1977). *A survival handbook for children of aging parents*. Chicago: Follett.

Shanas, E. (1960). Family responsibility and the health of older persons. *Journal of Gerontology, 15*, 408–411.

Shanas, E. (1962). *The health of older people: A social survey*. Cambridge, MA: Harvard University Press.

Shanas, E. (1978). Social myth as hypothesis: The case of family relations of older people. *The Gerontologist, 19,* 3–9.

Shedletsky, R. (1977). Behavior modification and the hospitalized elderly. *Essence, 2,* 25–31.

Sidman, M. (1960). *Tactics of scientific research*. New York: Basic Books.

Silverman, A. G., Kahn, B. H., & Anderson, G. A. (1977). A model for working with multi-generational families. *Social Casework, 58,* 131–135.

Silverstone, B., & Hyman, H. K. (1976). *You and your aging parent*. New York: Pantheon.

Skinner, B. F. (1983). Intellectual self-management in old age. *American Psychologist, 38,* 239–244.

Sussman, M. B. (1977). Family bureaucracy, and the elderly individual: An organizational/linkage perspective. In E. Shanas & M. B. Sussman (Eds.), *Family, bureaucracy, and the elderly*. Durham, NC: Duke University Press.

Sussman, M. B. (1965). Relationships of adult children with their parents in the United States. In E. Shanas & G. Streib (Eds.), *Social structure and the family: Generational relations*. Englewood Cliffs, NJ: Prentice-Hall.

Sussman, M. B. (1979, January). *Social and economic supports and family environments for the elderly*. Final report to the Administration on Aging.

Taepfer, C. T., Bucknell, A. T., & Shaw, D. O. (1974). Remotivation as behavior therapy. *The Gerontologist, 14,* 451–453.

Tharp, R. G., & Wetzel, R. J. (1969). *Behavior modification in the natural environment*. New York: Academic Press.

Tobin, S. S., & Lieberman, M. A. (1976). *Last home for the aged: Critical implication of institutionalization*. San Francisco: Jossey-Bass.

Townsend, P. (1965). The effects of family structure on the likelihood of admission to an institution in old age: The application of a general theory. In E. Shanas & G. F. Streib, (Eds.), *Social structure and the family: Generational relations*. Englewood Cliffs, NJ: Prentice-Hall.

Treas, J. (1977). Family support systems for the aged: Some social and demographic considerations. *The Gerontologist, 17,* 486–491.

Wahler, R. G. (1969). Oppositional children: A quest for parental reinforcement control. *Journal of Applied Behavior Analysis, 2,* 159–170.

Weissman, A. L. (1976). Industrial social services: Linkage technology. *Social Casework, 55,* 50–54.

Wheeler, G., & Knight, B. (1981). Morrie: A case study. *The Gerontologist, 21,* 323–328.

White House conference on aging. (1973). *Post White House conference on aging reports, 1973: Final report of the post-conference board of the 1971 White House conference on aging*. Washington, DC: U.S. Government Printing Office.

Woods, R. T., & Britton, P. G. (1977). Psychological approaches to the treatment of aging. *Age and Aging, 6,* 104–112.

Zarit, S. H., Reever, K. E., & Bachman Peterson, S. (1980). The burden interview. *The Gerontologist, 20,* 649–655.

Zarit, S. H., Reever, K. E., & Weston, J. A. (1980, November). *Working with families of the mentally impaired elderly*. Paper presented at the 33rd Annual Scientific Meeting of the Gerontological Society of America, San Diego.

Zimmer, A., Gross-Andrews, S., & Frankfather, D. (1977, November). *Incentives to families caring for disabled elderly*. Paper presented at the 30th Annual Scientific Meeting of the Gerontological Society of America, San Francisco.

Author Index

Adams, G. N., 98
Albanese, H., 8, 97, 101
Alford, B. A., 47, 104
Anderson, G. A., 7, 106
Atlas, L., 98, 99
Atthowe, J., 96
Ault, M. H., 26, 101
Azen, S. P., 98

Bachman Peterson, S., 31, 106
Baer, D. M., 26, 46, 51, 55, 99, 101, 105
Bardin-Ayers, S. K., 98
Baltes, M. M., 8, 9, 96, 98, 101
Barlow, D., 26, 51, 55, 57, 103
Barney, J. L., 6, 101
Barton, E. M., 9, 101
Bayne, J. R. D., 8, 101
Becker, W. C., 100
Bellucci, G., 10, 101
Bender, M. B., 31, 101
Benson, F. A. M., 104
Berger, R. M., 99
Berkowitz, B. P., 10, 99, 101
Bernal, M., 99
Bernstein, R., 9, 99, 101
Bijou, S. W., 26, 100, 101
Blackman, D. K., 8, 9, 37, 56, 96, 97, 98, 101, 105
Brandwein, B., 7, 102
Britton, P. G., 8, 106
Brody, E. M., 6, 102, 103
Brody, S., 6, 102
Brown, L. B., 102
Bucknell, A. T., 9, 99, 106
Budd, K. J., 100, 105

Bumagin, V. E., 7, 102
Burkhardt, J. E., 11, 102
Burns, B., 99
Busse, E. W., 6, 102
Bussink, T., 6, 102
Butler, A. K., 8, 97, 104
Butler, R. N., 6, 102

Caro, F. G., 71, 102
Cautela, J. R., 8, 102
Clark, F., 98
Clements, C., 97, 98
Cohen, D., 9, 99, 102
Cohen, S. Z., 7, 102
Collins, R., 96
Conger, R. E., 100
Corby, M., 99
Cordura, G., 41, 103
Costain, W. R., 7, 102
Cuvo, A. J., 97

Dangel, R. F., 100, 105
Dapcich-Miura, E., 98
de Vries, H. A., 98
Di Scipio, W., 97
Dvorkin, L., 9, 99, 101
Duryee, J. S., 99

Ebner, M. H., 10, 104
Edinberg, M. A., 99
Edwards, K. A., 96
Eisdorfer, C., 9, 99, 102
Epstein, L., 11, 102

Feldman, M., 97
Fink, M., 31, 101

Fischer, J., 34, 102
Forehand, R., 1
Frankel, R., 21, 102
Frankfather, D., 11, 102, 106
Frank, C. M., 103
Frekany, G. A., 98
Friedman, B. S., 10, 100, 105

Gaarder, K., 7, 97, 101
Gans, B. M., 7, 102
Gantry, W. D., 102
Gehle, C., 8, 96, 101
Geiger, D. G., 96
General Accounting Office, 6, 102
Giebenhain, J. E., 47, 104
Glesler, G., 99
Gochros, H. L., 34, 102
Goldberg, G., 11, 104
Goldfarb, A. I., 7, 28, 31, 102, 103
Goldiamond, I., 21, 23, 102, 105
Goldstein, A. P., 104
Goldstein, R. S., 99
Grad de Alarcon, J., 7, 102
Graziano, A. M., 10, 99, 101
Green, G. R., 10, 34, 41, 60, 70, 96, 99, 100, 102, 104, 105
Green, M., 31, 101
Greenley, J. R., 11, 103
Grinnell, R. M., 103
Grosicki, J. P., 8, 96, 103
Gross-Andrews, S., 7, 106

Haley, W. E., 7, 103
Hayden, M., 41, 103
Hall, R. V., 55, 103
Hawkins, R. P., 100
Haynes, S. N., 97
Herbert-Jackson, E. W., 41, 100, 103
Hersen, M., 26, 51, 55, 57, 103
Hirn, K. F., 7, 102
Hoelhe, A., 97
Howe, M. W., 8, 9, 37, 96, 98, 101, 103, 104
Howell, M. F., 98
Hoyer, F. W., 9, 98, 99, 103
Hoyer, W. J., 8, 9, 10, 98, 99, 101, 103, 105

Hudson, W. W., 103
Hughston, G. A., 7, 103
Hussian, R. A., 8, 103
Hyman, H. K., 7, 106

Jackson, C., 41, 103
Jackson, G. M., 8, 97, 103
Jacobi, J. N., 85
Jason, L. A., 99
Jayaratne, S., 51, 55, 103
Johnson, C. A., 10, 100, 103
Johnson, L. A., 96
Jones, R. R., 100

Kafer, R. A., 9, 98, 99, 103
Kahn, B. H., 7, 106
Kahn, R. L., 3, 31, 103
Kahn, R. S., 103
Kanfer, F. H., 103, 104
Karoly, P., 99
Kastenbaum, R., 8, 97, 103, 104
Katz, R. A., 10, 100, 103
Keckich, W., 102
Keller, J. F., 7, 103
Kirk, S. A., 11, 103
Kleban, M. H., 31, 103
Knight, B., 10, 106
Kochman, A., 100
Kohn, J. P., 97
Koncelik, J. A., 97
Kosberg, J. I., 7, 103, 104
Kratochwill, T. R., 55, 103
Kucherawy, D. A., 98
Kulys, R., 6, 103

Lascomb, S. L., 96, 98
Lav, E. E., 7, 104
Lawton, M. P., 31, 103
Levenstein, P., 100
Leslie, D. K., 98
Levendusky, P. G., 9, 104
Levit, G., 6, 104
Levitt, J. L., 10, 104, 105
Levy, R., 51, 55, 103
Lewis, M. I., 6, 102
Libb, J. W., 97, 98
Liberman, M. A., 106

Lieberman, R. P., 6, 7, 96
Lindsley, O. R., 8, 20, 36, 104
Linsk, N. L., 9, 10, 37, 41, 92, 94, 96, 98, 99, 102, 104, 105, 107
Lloyd, K. E., 97
Longin, H. E., 97
Lopez, M. A., 99

Mabry, J., 101
MacDonald, M. L., 8, 97, 98, 104
Macurik, K. M., 97
Maddox, G. L., 6, 104
Mansfield, L., 8, 102
Masciocchi, C., 6, 102
Meichenbaum, D., 10, 104
Melamed, B. G., 10, 104
Middleman, R., 11, 104
Miller, L. R., 98
Minahan, A., 11, 105
Mishara, B. L., 8, 9, 97, 103, 104
Morris, R., 7, 104
Mueller, D. J., 98, 99
McCauley, D. C., 21, 102
McClannahan, L. E., 8, 9, 98, 104
McDearmon, J. R., 98

Nay, W. R., 45, 104
Nesselroade, J., 105

O'Briant, A. L., 47, 104
O'Dell, S., 10, 47, 100, 104
O'Leary, K. D., 100
O'Quin, J. A., 47, 104
Otten, J., 7, 104

Page, F. I., 8, 104
Patterson, G. R., 1, 10, 100, 104
Peck, R., 31, 103
Peterson, R. F., 27, 100, 101
Pfieffer, E., 31, 102, 105
Pierce, C. H., 98
Pincus, A., 11, 105
Pinkston, E. M., 1, 8, 9, 10, 14, 20, 26, 34, 37, 41, 53, 92, 94, 95, 96, 98, 99, 100, 101, 102, 103, 104, 105, 107
Pinkston, S., 41, 103
Plaska, T., 96

Pollack, D. D., 96
Pollock, M., 103
Polster, R. A., 10, 100, 105
Postoff, R., 7, 102
Potter, R. E., 98
Poulshock, W., 6, 102
Premack, D., 38, 105
Preston, C., 9, 99, 102
Prince, M. G., 97
Proppe, H., 97
Pruett, H. I., 99

Quattrochi-Tubin, S., 99

Rankin, E. R., 105
Rapoport, R., 7, 105
Rapoport, R. N., 7, 105
Rathbone-McCuzn, E., 7, 105
Rebok, G. W., 8, 105
Reese, H., 105
Reever, K. E., 7, 31, 106
Reid, J. B., 100
Reid, W. J., 11, 55, 102, 105
Reidel, R. G., 8, 9, 103
Rinke, C. L., 97
Risley, T. R., 8, 26, 55, 98, 101, 104, 105
Robertson, B., 8, 97, 104
Rose, S. D., 99
Roth, H., 100
Rzepnicki, T. L., 104, 105

Sachs, D. A., 97, 99
Safford, F., 7, 105
Sager, A., 12, 105
Sainsbury, P., 7, 102
Sajwasj, T., 41, 103
Saslow, G., 14, 103
Schier, B., 7, 105
Schinke, S. P., 100, 105
Schipke, J., 76
Schwartz, A., 8, 21, 97, 105
Schwartz, A. N., 7, 105
Schweld, E., 100
Settin, J. M., 98
Shanas, E., 6, 31, 102, 105, 106
Shaw, D. A., 10, 104

Shaw, D. O., 9, 106
Shedletsky, R., 8, 106
Shelley, F. D., 7, 104
Sherwood, S., 104
Siegel, L. J., 104
Sidman, M., 57, 106
Simpson, S. C., 9, 98, 99, 103
Simmons, J. B., 97
Siverstone, B., 7, 106
Silverman, A. G., 7, 106
Skinner, B. F., 8, 106
Smith, A. D., 55, 105
Smith, M. J., 7, 102
Smith-Scott, W., 97
Snyder, L., 97
Stachnik, T., 101
Stamford, B. A., 98
Streib, G. F., 102, 106
Strelitz, Z., 7, 105
Sussman, M. B., 6, 7, 11, 106

Taepfer, C. T., 9, 99, 106
Taylor, C. B., 97
Tharp, R. G., 10, 106
Thomas, J. A., 98
Tobin, S. S., 6, 7, 103, 106

Toseland, R. W., 99
Townsend, P., 6, 106
Treas, J., 6, 7, 106

Ulrich, R., 101

Van Der Tak, J., 6, 102

Wahler, R. G., 41, 106
Weissman, A. L., 11, 37, 49, 106
Weston, J. A., 7, 106
Wetzel, R. J., 10, 106
Wheeler, G., 10, 106
White House Conference on Aging,
   7, 106
Williams, J. J., 97
Wolf, M. M., 26, 46, 55, 101, 105
Woods, R. T., 8, 106

Young, R. N., 68, 79, 96

Zarit, S. H., 7, 31, 79, 106
Zerbe, M. B., 8, 101
Zimmer, A., 7, 106
Zlotnick, S. I., 97
Zuga, C. S., 6, 102

Subject Index

Activity levels (increasing), 70
ADL (activities of daily living),
  evaluation, 70
  intervention plans, 66–69, 70
Alzheimer's Type, Senile Dementia,
  76–79
Arthritis, 1
Assessment, 33
  behavioral interview, 20–21
    problem assessment, 20–21
    problem selection, 21
  component analysis, 20
  direct measures, 26–29
  indirect measures, 29–32
    pre-post assessments, 31
  observation, 24–29
    anecdotal record, 25
    observation code, 26–27
      frequency, 27
      duration, 27
      latency, 27
      reliability, 27–29

Behavioral family training, 42, 99–100
Behavioral gerontology, 7–9
Behavior change strategies (ap-
    proaches), 35–39, 58–90,
    98–99
  decreasing behaviors, 39, 64–73,
    82–83, 83–84, 85–90
  delivery system, 43–44
  educating caregivers, 41–43
    didatic, 42
    modeling, 42
    feedback, 43
    reinforcement, 43

goals, individualized, 35
increasing opportunities for reinforcement, 36
increasing behaviors, 38, 58–64,
  76–79, 98–99
increasing social contact, 58–64
  intervention procedures, 59
  practice illustration, 60–64
stimulus cueing, 64–73
  self-care, 64–69
  activity record, 70
  elimination program (urinary in-
    continence), 69–73
  prompts, 65
  task assignment, 62
  task assignment work sheet, 62
Behavior change strategies, 35–50,
    See also Intervention pro-
    cedures
Behavioral model, 13–32, 92–93
  assessment, 13–32
  bibliography, 96–100
  intervention, 33–50
  termination, 49–50
  maintenance, 44–49
  follow-up, 49
    availability of practitioner, 50
    telephone, 50
Behavioral paradigm, 14, 15
  antecedent events, 15
  consequences, 15
  functional analysis, 14
  prosthetic environment, 20
Behavior problems (practice illustra-
    tions), 70–100
  activity, 70

Behavior problems (*continued*)
  Alzheimer's type, senile dementia,
    76–79
  ambulation, 97
  clinical depression, 80
  eating, 96
  elimination, 69
  isolation, 58
  manic depressive illness, 69
  medical regimens, 98
  multiple problem example, 79–85
    personal care, 66–69, 81, 97
    aggression and socialization, 82
    household chores, 83
    intrusive family contacts, 84
  paranoid, 60
  physical exercise, 98
  relocation, 61–62
  self-care, 64–69, 96–97
  social, 58–64, 99
  urinary incontinence, 68–73, 96
  verbal behavior, 73–79, 98–97
Behavioral treatment. *See also*
    Intervention procedures

Caregivers, 20
  assessment, 16–20
  criteria for selection, 3–4
  burden, 31
  characteristics, 3, 4, 17
  checklist, 17–19
  interviewing, 21
  referral procedure, 17
Client selection, 3
Clinical depression, 69. *See also*
    Behavior problems
Community service, 47–49
  linkages, 47–49
  linkage procedures, 49
  sources of service, 49
  when to link, 48

Diabetes, 66
  urine check (blood sugar), 66

Eating, 96
Economic resources, 31

Education (caregiver), 41–43
Emotional disturbances. *See*
    Behavioral problems
Environmental factors. *See* Behavioral
    paradigm
Excess disability (definition), 3

Face-hand tests, 31
Family, *See* Caregivers and
    Behavioral change strategies;
    educating caregivers
Family behavior record, 30

Goals, 35
Group activities, 98

Hallucinations, 85

Incontinence (urinary), 69–73, 96
Intervention procedures, 33–39, 60–90
    (practice illustrations),
    96–100. *See also* Behavioral
    intervention strategies, 33–50,
    58–90
  attention and feedback, 43
  component behaviors, 39
  contingent reinforcement, 38–39
  contracting, 43
  differential attention, 40
  environmental cues, 37
  guidelines for selecting reinforcers,
    38
  increasing cues, 36
  increasing incompatible behavior,
    40
  increasing opportunities for rein-
    forcement, 36, 39
  increasing social opportunities, 37
  intervention selection guide, 42
  token economies, 44
Interviewing, 21

Maintenance of change, 44–47
  fading, 45
  environmental reprogramming, 46
  planned, 44
  program transfer, 47

Medical regimens, 98
Memory, 99
Mental status tests, 31

Orientation. *See* Behavioral change
    strategies; stimulus cueing

Paranoid disorder, 60
Personal care, 97
Person-environment. *See* Behavioral
    paradigm
Physical exercise, 98
Physical health, 20
Physical illness, 20
Physical pathology, 20
Privacy (intrusive contacts), 84
Pre-post assessment. *See* Assessment;
    indirect measures
Problem behaviors. *See* Behavior
    problems
Prosthetic environment, 20
Psychological tests. *See* Assessment;
    indirect measures

Relocation, 60–64
Repetitive speech, 73–79, 98–99

Repetitive movement, 97
Research programs, clinical, 7–11,
    96–100

Self-care skills, 64–69, 96–97
Self-injurious behaviors, 97
Self-report scales. *See* Assessment;
    direct measures
Senile dementia. *See* Alzheimer's
    type
Single-case designs, 53–57
    clinical criteria design, 53, 54
    intervention-reversal design, 53
    changing criteria design, 53, 54
    multiple-baseline-across-behaviors
        design, 54, 55
    multiple-baseline-across-settings
        design, 54, 56
    multiple-replication design, 54, 56
Social behaviors, 99
Social resources, 47–49
    community services, 47–49

Urinary incontinence. *See* Incontinence

Verbal behavior, 73–79, 98–99

About the Authors

Elsie M. Pinkston (PhD, The University of Kansas) is an Associate Professor at the School of Social Service Administration, The University of Chicago, and the Principal Investigator of The Elderly Support Project. She chaired the Applied Behavior Analysis Sequence at The University of Chicago and currently teaches advanced clinical practice there. During the past 10 years she was also the principal investigator of several family treatment research grants developing procedures for behavioral family therapy, particularly with families who have special caregiving problems, such as mentally and physically impaired elderly members or children with behavior problems. Her work was published in the *Journal of Applied Behavior Analysis, Social Work, Social Service Review, Social Work Research and Abstracts,* and *The Gerontologist.* She is the first author of *Effective Social Work Practice.* Dr. Pinkston serves on the editorial boards of several journals and is a member of the Human Development and Aging Review Committee of the National Institutes of Health.

Nathan L. Linsk (PhD, The University of Chicago) is Assistant Professor at the College of Associated Health Professions, the University of Illinois, and a senior coordinator in the Department of Medical Social Work. He was the Director of the Elderly Support Project at the University of Chicago from 1979–1984. His 11 years of direct practice experience with the elderly and his research and practice interest include behavioral family intervention, behavioral group work with the elderly, professional supervision and training, long-term care policy and community advocacy, and empirically based practice education. He has published in *Social Work* and *The Gerontologist* and is a coauthor of *Effective Social Work Practice.* He consults with the Veterans Administration and the Illinois Citizens for Better Care.

Psychology Practitioner Guidebooks

Editors:
Arnold P. Goldstein, Syracuse University
Leonard Krasner, SUNY at Stony Brook
Sol L. Garfield, Washington University

Edward B. Blanchard & Frank Andrasik – *MANAGEMENT OF CHRONIC HEADACHES: A Psychological Approach*

Philip H. Bornstein & Marcy T. Bornstein – *MARITAL THERAPY: A Behavioral-Communications Approach*

Karen S. Calhoun & Beverly M. Atkeson – *TREATMENT OF VICTIMS OF SEXUAL ASSAULT*

Richard F. Dangel & Richard A. Polster – *TEACHING OF CHILD MANAGEMENT SKILLS*

Donald Meichenbaum – *STRESS-INOCULATION TRAINING*

Michael T. Nietzel & Ronald C. Dillehay – *PSYCHOLOGICAL CONSULTATION IN THE COURTROOM*

Elsie M. Pinkston & Nathan L. Linsk – *CARE OF THE ELDERLY: A Family Approach*

Raymond G. Romanczyk – *CLINICAL UTILIZATION OF MICRO-COMPUTER TECHNOLOGY*

Sebastiano Santostefano – *COGNITIVE CONTROL THERAPY WITH CHILDREN AND ADOLESCENTS*

Elizabeth Yost, Larry E. Beutler, Anne Corbishley & James Allender – *GROUP COGNITIVE THERAPY: A Treatment Method for the Depressed Elderly*